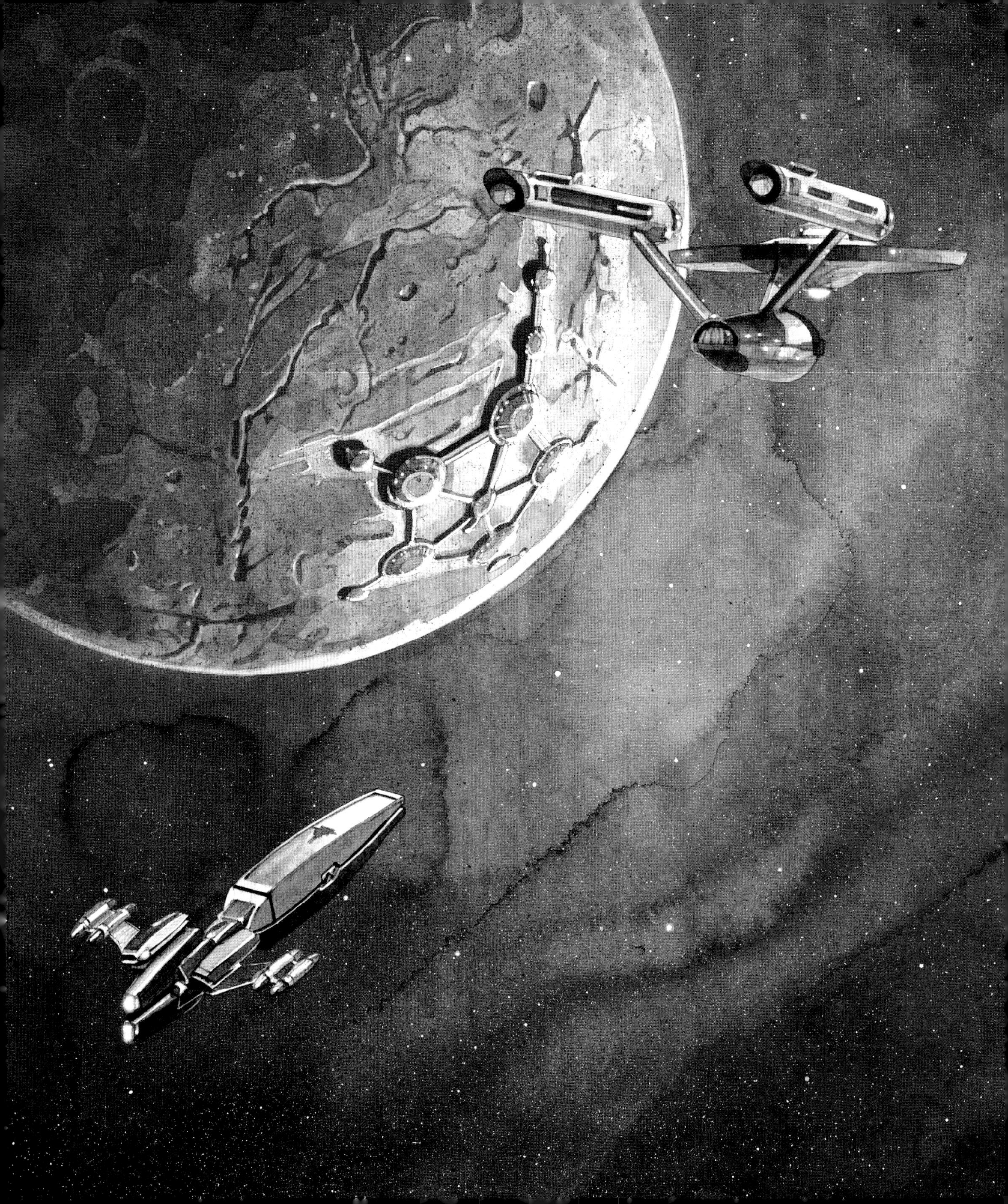

FEDERATION

The First 150 Years

David A. Goodman

To Talia, Jacob,
and Wendy

CONTENTS

A NOTE ON SOURCES

The following history was commissioned by the Council of the United Federation of Planets to celebrate the 150th anniversary of its founding. The true story that follows is based on first-person interviews, official documents, letters, personal and official logs, journalistic accounts, and memoirs. Many sources were already in the care of the researchers at the Federation Library on Memory Alpha. Other material was gathered through visits to the archives of the Federation member worlds, including the Vulcan Science Academy, the War College of the Andorian High Command, and the Klingon High Council, as well as many of the Federation's starships and starbases, colonies, and outposts.

David A. Goodman
Memory Alpha Historian

PROLOGUE

COCHRANE'S FLIGHT

2063–2120

"Don't try to be a great man, just be a man. Let history make its own judgments."

—Zefram Cochrane, 2073

OPPOSITE: Zefram Cochrane's warp-drive prototype, the *Phoenix*.

The two figures met on a chilly April evening near a missile silo in northern Montana. They were from different worlds, Earth and Vulcan, and this was the first open contact between the two species (Vulcans, it was later discovered, had been visiting Earth in secret for centuries). They introduced themselves to each other in the greetings common on their worlds; the Vulcan offered his salute, the Human, a handshake.

"I didn't know what I was supposed to do," the Human would say in an interview years later. "The truth was I was pretty drunk."

It was an introduction without fanfare, but it would prove significant in the annals of diplomacy; aliens from across the quadrant would honor the date, April 5, "First Contact Day," as one of the only intergalactic holidays. Though the other founding member races of the Federation—the Andorians, the Tellarites, and the Vulcans—had already had their own "first contacts" with one another previous to this, they would honor this day specifically because they understood that without this meeting there would have been no Federation.

But it was still a prologue; the formation of an intergalactic union was a very long way off. When these two beings met, they did not talk about trade or alliances. Neither one felt he had the authority, the legitimacy, or the necessity to speak for anyone but himself. The Human, Zefram Cochrane, and the Vulcan, Solkar, did not, nor could not, foresee the effect their actions would have on the Galaxy. They were products of their worlds, closed societies whose intermingling would change both their home planets' populations, as well as those of dozens of other worlds.

Zefram Cochrane was born on January 27, 2031, into a society that for decades had not known a moment's peace. The wars began in 1992, when genetically enhanced men and women came to power in countries around the world during what would be known as the "Eugenics Wars," the first stage of World War III. Historian John Gill, whose multi-volume history of World War III is the definitive work on the subject, wrote: "In four catastrophic years, these genetic supermen seized control with the use of nuclear weapons. They devastated populations and permanently redrew the map of the world." *

North, Central, and South America became the American Empire under the dictator Asahf Ferris; Australia, New Zealand, and the Pacific Islands fell under the rule of Bernard Maltuvis; Europe was ruled by John Ericssen; and Asia through the Middle East, dubbed the Eastern Coalition, was under the control of Khan Noonien Singh.

OPPOSITE: An artist's rendition of the meeting of Cochrane and Solkar on April 5, 2063, known colloquially throughout the Federation as "First Contact." The original currently hangs in the Hall of the Federation Council. ***AUTHOR'S NOTE:** Indeed, the legacy of the Eugenics Wars is so severe and horrific, shortly after it became public that time travel was possible, many people thought it would be worth going back in time and changing this chapter in Human history. In 2293, one terrorist group of Humans took action: calling itself "1992," they stole the *U.S.S. Yorktown* from the Starfleet museum and attempted to return to the past and erase these events from Earth's history. They disappeared without a trace along with their ship. Because we believe we are all living in an unchanged history, if they were successful it was only in creating an alternate timeline.

MEMORY ALPHA LCARS HARD COPY EXTRACT

ORIGINAL SOURCE: UNITED ASSOCIATION PRESS	17.9.1996

MYSTERY COMMANDOES STEAL ADVANCED SPACESHIP

By Sarah Jane Smith

JIUQUAN, GANSU CHINA—In a daring and bloody pre-dawn raid, a mysterious group of intruders attacked Jiuquan Satellite Base and stole a DY-100 spaceship, successfully launching it at 2:30am today. There are few clues to the identity of the perpetrators, who left fifteen people dead and thirty-three wounded in their assault on the secluded satellite and spaceship launch complex located in China's Gobi Desert.

"It's one thing to attack the base, but the idea that people could just hop into one of our most advanced spaceships and take off is unbelievable," said Chao Jyalin, Director of Operations for the base. "This isn't like stealing a car." The DY-100 is the state of the art in spaceship design. One of the many "sleeper ships" commissioned by the dictator Khan Noonien Singh, the spacecrafts are capable of holding a hundred people in suspended animation, allowing for journeys of longer duration than previously possible in space travel. In the years since their introduction, the ships and their crews have set up automated mining facilities on Mars and in the Asteroid Belt.

Another mystery surrounding the theft of the craft is that one of the survivors said he saw the perpetrators paint a name on the side of the craft. "I got hit on the back of the head," Lin Haur, a security guard at the facility stated, "and when I came to, the rocket was launching. I could see they had painted a name on the side. Looked like a couple of English words." Though Lin Haur couldn't read English, investigators asked him to draw the word, which appeared to be "Botany." No one at the base or among the investigative team has yet found any meaning in this.

Tracking systems on Earth quickly lost track of the ship once it launched. "It's left Earth's orbit, we're sure of that," said Victor Bergman, chief astronomer at the Anderson Space Command, "but it's got to come back at some point. There just isn't anywhere else to go."

"Their control did not last long," Gill wrote, "because their oversized ambitions led them to war with one another." This weakened their holds on their populations and allowed resistance movements the opportunity to overthrow them.

"But their devastating effect on the world was permanent," Gill wrote, "and peace would elude the new nations that were left in their wake."

At the time of Cochrane's birth, civilization continued to deteriorate, and, with a few blips of hope, careened headlong into barbarism. In 2037, NASA was re-established and had launched the *Charybdis*, a manned extra-solar probe. But only a few years later the forces of anti-intellectualism took root in the former United States (now part of a failing democracy that included Central and South America) and in 2044, responding to the public unrest, the government ordered a purge of academia. Cochrane's parents, two academics at the University of Chicago, were killed, and, as a teenage orphan, he was forced to learn how to survive on his own in a world ravaged by war, famine, and climate change.

"My parents raised me to be an intellectual," Cochrane wrote in his autobiography. "They wanted me to be naturally curious and analytical. But when they were gone, the violent anti-intellectualism of society forced me to hide these tendencies." He became a pragmatist. His desire to study science was only accepted in one arena: the conduct of war. So he found work at one of the last outposts of scientific research, working for a military contractor.

The planet, meanwhile, was moving inexorably close to the second stage of World War III. The conflicts of the past had reduced the amount of livable land; food and energy were at a premium. In 2051, Le Kuan, a general in the armed forces of the Eastern Coalition, overthrew a tottering democracy. Though he wasn't genetically engineered, Kuan was still brutal and ambitious. Faced with a starving population and dwindling resources, he launched an attack on the Americas in an attempt to increase his holdings. Europe, under the governance of the European Hegemony, sided with the Americas; the Pacific nations joined with Kuan; and the final stage of World War III began in earnest.

Throughout the conflict, Cochrane found himself designing and developing anti-matter weapons. "I was fascinated

FIG A - DILITHIUM

LEFT: Unrefined dilithium crystals. **OPPOSITE:** A UAP news article reported the theft of the ship that would eventually be named the *S.S. Botany Bay*. It would be two centuries before the fate of the ship was discovered; it carried almost one hundred genetically engineered supermen and -women into the twenty-third century, where they would create more havoc, and more deaths.

by matter/anti-matter reactions, and this was the only way I could get access to the latest research." Cochrane was especially intrigued by the reports of an element called dilithium, excavated near the South Pole, where astrogeologists had been discovering extraterrestrial material in meteorites since the twentieth century.

"The more I learned about this crystal that wasn't native to Earth," Cochrane wrote, "the more it seemed to hold the answer to regulating the very unstable reaction of a theoretical matter/anti-matter reactor." This was his secret breakthrough, leading to his design of what would become the first warp engine.

Revisionist historians have postulated that Cochrane purposely kept it out of the hands of the dictators who ruled his world, but a more honest examination of the man can't ignore the one quote Cochrane gave on the topic. "I was an opportunist," he said in an interview. "I kept my discovery to myself until I could figure out a way to make money off of it."

While bombs dropped and troops from the differing factions attempted to take what little valuable land was left, Cochrane bided his time, assembling a trusted circle of technicians, engineers, and scientists. An engineer named Lily Sloane was one of Cochrane's first recruits. "He was frustrating; on the one hand he was so irresponsible, he drank so much," Sloane said, in a biography of Cochrane, "but he had this vision, and it gave you hope, so I found myself doing what he wanted."

In 2053, a strike by American forces destroyed the governing palace of the Eastern Coalition, killing Le Kuan. His replacement, his son Le Yu, immediately sued for peace. The leaders of the world sent delegates to San Francisco, one of the few major cities untouched by the war, to hammer out their cease-fire agreement (the United Nations Headquarters having been destroyed along with the rest of Manhattan). They met in a building on the Presidio, which had once been a United States military installation before it was shut down and leased to private businesses, including a producer of science fiction movies. The peace treaty written there that ended WWIII was far from perfect (Gill pointed out that it greatly overreacted on the subject of Human genetic engineering, limiting untold benefits from future medical advancements) but it established a diplomatic infrastructure that remained in place for many years following its signing.

The war finally over, Cochrane quietly made his move. He had a computer expert erase the location of an already secret missile silo in Montana from all military records, then moved his ragtag group there, with the promise that this venture would make them all wealthy. "We were like a rogue 'Manhattan Project,'" Sloane said. "Not only were we forced to scrounge what Zee [her nickname for Cochrane] needed for his project, we also needed food and water."

OPPOSITE: This excerpt from the Treaty of San Francisco signed in 2055 details the banning of all genetic engineering of the Human genome. Though the Eugenics Wars were already decades in the past, it speaks to the long-lasting effect they had on Earth and, by extension, the Federation. A slightly altered version of this clause would eventually become part of both the Constitution of Earth's world government and, much later, the Federation Charter.

PART XVIII

GENETIC ENGINEERING OF THE HUMAN GENOME

GENERAL PROVISIONS

ARTICLE 618

The Allied and Associated powers, recognizing the destructive role genetic engineering of the human genome played in the recent conflict, agree to collectively limit and control all such research in this area, and ban any practical application of such research. This includes, but is not limited to, the purposeful or accidental manipulation of DNA in a grown human being, or said manipulation of DNA in the creation of a human being. Such purposeful or accidental results of the manipulation of DNA banned by this treaty include, but are not limited to: increased muscle or skin density, enhanced brain function, superior immune system, and enhanced ocular, olfactory, auditory, somatosensory, or gustatory functions.

ARTICLE 619

The Allied and Associated powers agree to destroy all but ten (10) percent of all genetically enhanced materials seized during the conflict. Recognizing that this material may provide necessary medical or scientific information at some undetermined future date, the portion that is not destroyed shall be placed in secure storage. The storage facility shall be in a location to be determined by mutual agreement of the Allied and Associated powers, and said facility shall be jointly run by said powers.

4/12/56

We stand in this protective bubble on the ~~war-torn~~ ruins of Washington, D.C., once the center of power for the greatest nation on Earth. Behind me once stood the U.S. Capitol building, where democracy flourished and inspired other peoples to their ideals. Now, it is gone. And across the world our brothers in Europe and Asia and Africa face their own personal devastations at the landmarks to human culture that have been destroyed in this war. My heart goes out to them.

In the shadow of this *incalculable* devastation, we find ourselves facing a colossal challenge. There is an entire world to rebuild. Not only our cities and homes, but mankind itself. Now is not the time for timidity and second-guessing. We cannot afford to doubt ourselves. Unless we act decisively, we will pass on the scars of mutation and decay to future generations. ~~For the sake of our children, and our children's children, we must reject the impure and cast it out~~.

I therefore, ~~despite resistance from the other allied leaders,~~ *in conjunction with the leaders of the combined allied forces all over the world* order today, protocols for the weeding out of those individuals affected by exposure to nuclear radiation.

The first protocol: The establishment of the World Medical Organization. As of this moment, all medical facilities around the world have already responded to this body's first order of reporting: a detailed listing from every medical facility and physician or medic of every human being who has experienced radiation exposure.

The second protocol: The world's Allied Command will immediately begin relocation of affected individuals to a secure *undisclosed* location.

The third protocol: Once relocated, sterilization will commence immediately.

The fourth protocol: During relocation, all property belonging to those deemed necessary for sterilization shall be seized by Allied Command for cataloguing and eventual redistribution.

or will be handed over to remaining family members

Cochrane and his team turned the missile in the silo into Earth's first warp-drive vessel. "It took a decade, which doesn't seem so long," Sloane said, "but if we'd been building a weapon with funding from a government, it would have only been a couple of years."

Cochrane had chosen his location well. Throughout the end of the war and Earth's tentative peace, the team was able to live undisturbed, allowing them to finish the project. On April 5, 2063, Cochrane piloted his refurbished missile, christened the *Phoenix*, past the speed of light. He and his team had little time to plan how they would cash in, because Cochrane's return to Earth brought a piece of the Galaxy with him: the Vulcan Solkar.

If, as John Gill said, Cochrane's flight "was the work of an extraordinary man fighting upstream against the flow of his own planet's history," then the work of Cochrane's counterpart from Vulcan was the exact opposite: Solkar was a common Vulcan living a common Vulcan life.

1,400 years before, the Vulcans had been a violent and savage race, engaged in conflicts that could have led to their destruction. From out of this cauldron came Surak, Vulcan's greatest philosopher. "Surak recognized that violence came from emotions," wrote Syran, a well-known follower of Surak, "and therefore only by rejecting all emotions and embracing a philosophy of logic would Vulcan be able to survive."

Surak was a victim of the conflicts he sought to end. He died of radiation poisoning and did not live to see his people eventually embrace his philosophy. But by the time Humanity encountered the Vulcans, they were a peaceful, advanced, extremely orderly society, and Solkar reflected that. He was the son of an astrophysicist/biologist, as he himself had become. He gained admission to the Vulcan Science Academy just as his ancestors had and his descendants would. The Vulcan High Command assigned him to the science vessel *T'plana-Hath* at the age of sixty (though several decades older than Cochrane, he looked a good deal younger), which was considered a logical age to assume command of an exploratory team. He took his ship on the prescribed course through the prescribed systems, formally adhering to strict codes of scientific conduct. When his ship's sensors detected the *Phoenix* traveling at Warp 1.1, piloted by a species that, according to the Vulcan database, did not have warp drive, there was no decision for Solkar to make. The standard procedures laid out by the High Command gave a ship's commanding officer only one choice for this contingency: Solkar was to investigate and report back. So he landed his

OPPOSITE: Though the Third World War had finally come to an end, the horrors weren't over. After the war, Colonel Philip Green, one of the leaders of the Western Alliance, instituted his own draconian measures. In an attempt to "purify" Humanity, he ordered the deaths of those Humans deemed "nuclear mutations." Hundreds of thousands died before he himself was overthrown. **FOLLOWING SPREAD:** The Vulcan philosopher Surak grew up in a world plagued by war and on the edge of self-destruction. As a young man, he fought in those wars in the infantry; he attributed much of his later philosophy to the changes he underwent during this ordeal. In this section from the original first draft manuscript of his teachings, Surak relays his experience in escaping from captivity into the Forge, an area of Vulcan decimated by nuclear war. This was the beginning of his pilgrimage; his experience there would shape his attitudes toward emotions.

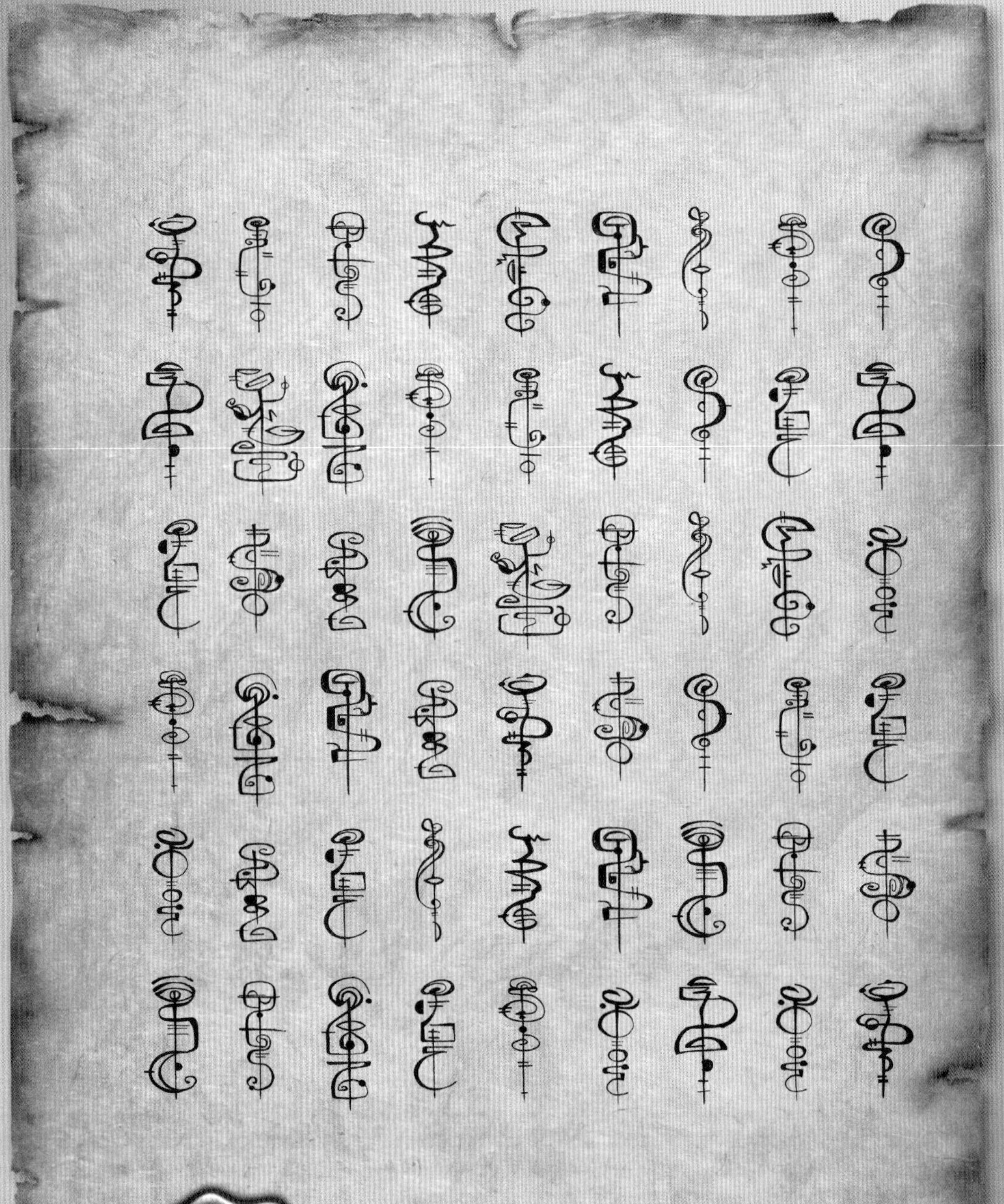

AN EXCERPT FROM THE TEACHINGS OF SURAK

TRANSLATED FROM THE VULCAN

. . . I was sick over my humiliation; I had succumbed to their torture, given them all the information they had sought, and even some they had not thought to ask. When I escaped, they needed to expend no energy in trying to find me. I had run into the Forge, where nothing could survive.

It would be years before the radiation sickness I contracted in the Forge would kill me, but kill me it would. Even then, I knew this, but I still somehow hoped that I would survive. During my long trek in the Forge, I thought about hope, and realized hope is fear; it is the mind's desire to deny what it knows to be true and unpleasant. Hope is fear.

I traveled at night and dreamed of the comfort of home . . . but yet, I knew I could not return there. The thought of my betrayal brought guilt, and I knew I could never go home; the guilt was too powerful. I thought about guilt, and realized guilt is also fear; fear that what I had done would deprive me of love. Guilt is fear.

I continued on into the Forge, two days without water, three days . . . one morning I was awakened by the sound of a flying warcraft losing control and crashing. I ran to the wreck. The two pilots inside were dead, but I pulled their bodies from the wreckage anyway, before the craft finally exploded. I sat with the bodies for a long time. They had no water, but thirst was overcoming me, and I thought . . . I could drink their blood. It would allow me to survive.

My religious upbringing considered this a violation of sacred law. If I did this and was discovered, I would be an outcast, I would be tried and executed. I won't tell them, I thought; no one would know. But what if they found out?

I considered. What was I afraid of? The dead bodies would be taken by the ground. Their blood would allow me to live a little longer. But why did I need to live longer? I could not go home. But then I realized I had to go home, even with the guilt. My family wants me home. I loved my family, and they loved me. I knew this was real love. But would my family still love me if they'd known I drank the blood of the dead to survive? Would they still love me knowing I had betrayed my comrades? I was trapped in indecision.

I saw for the first time that you could not have love without fear. Love, true love—not love motivated by carnal pleasure, but love motivated by a need for emotional connection—is a force for good; it leads to generosity and compassion. But fear stalks in love's shadow, and uses love for its own ends. When love is real, fear of the loss of that love is always nearby. You cannot have good emotions without bringing the bad ones along.

I stepped back from my indecision; like a cool breath, logic took over and told me to survive. I drank the blood, buried the bodies, and continued on.

ship at the coordinates where the warp ship was launched, and that night experienced his first glass of bourbon.

Although history books have often portrayed the first contact as a civilized meeting of great minds, Lily Sloane described a far less rarefied and auspicious event. "Zee took him into the bar we'd set up, and tried to get him drunk," Sloane said, "but the Vulcans could hold their liquor, and they didn't get drunk.

"Then Zee put on music and started to dance. The Vulcans weren't having any of it." Solkar offered to give Cochrane a tour of his ship, and Cochrane, now seriously inebriated, asked if there were any Vulcan women on board. When Solkar said there weren't, Cochrane decided he wasn't interested and returned to the bar, continuing to drink until he passed out.

"Zee's passed out on a table," Sloane wrote. "The Vulcans are looking at me; I don't know what to do. And then I didn't have to do anything, because a couple of helicopters started circling around." The Vulcans got in their ship and left.

BELOW: The Vulcan ship *T'plana-Hath*, in San Francisco. **OPPOSITE:** The *New New York Times* headline announces Cochrane's historic flight and the arrival of the Vulcans. Though the original *New York Times* was destroyed along with the city during the Eugenics Wars, New New York was established on its ruins, and surviving journalists sought to at least temporarily resurrect the illustrious paper of record.

THE NEW NEW YORK TIMES

April 6, 2063

Humans go faster than light, make contact with aliens

"They look a lot like the devil," *says eyewitness*

BOZEMAN, MONTANA—In an incredible confluence of history-making events, a Montana man named Zefram Cochrane launched a homemade spaceship from a nuclear missile silo yesterday and traveled faster than the speed of light, effectively rewriting the laws of physics.

The flight prompted humanity's first contact with aliens from another planet, when an alien spaceship observed Mr. Cochrane's flight and followed his spaceship back to Earth.

This remarkable event affirms the existence of intelligent life beyond Earth. According to witnesses, the aliens call themselves "Vulcans." They bear a strong resemblance to human beings, differentiated only by a greenish tint to their skin color, pointed ears, and slanted eyebrows.

"They look like Halloween versions of Satan," Mr. Cochrane said after spending several hours with them, "but act like distant British schoolmasters." Apparently, although they speak a native Vulcan language, they have observed Earth for many centuries and all three occupants of the craft spoke English, as well as several other human languages, with fluency.

Both ships were picked up on tracking systems all over the world. Mr. Cochrane's ship, a refurbished ICBM installed with a matter/anti-matter reactor of Mr. Cochrane's design, flew for one minute at a little past the speed of light (more specifics about the unique history of Mr. Cochrane's ship and flight on page A10). A few hours after both ships returned to Earth, the American military sent helicopters to the area.

"I flew over the silo," Frank Christopher, a lieutenant in the Army Air Force, said. "There was this giant thing that looked like a cathedral sitting there."

Lt. Christopher did not, however, get to meet the aliens. "While I was circling, the cathedral craft lifted off. Its backwash almost knocked me out of the sky. Still trying to wrap my mind around the whole thing."

THE VULCAN STEWARDSHIP

Solkar didn't go far. He went into orbit and reported back to Vulcan. The information he and his crew had gathered convinced the High Command that Earth needed more in-depth study. And because he'd made the first contact, the High Command immediately appointed Solkar the first ambassador to Earth ("Logically," Solkar said later to his grandson Sarek, "I knew more about the current Earth situation than any of my colleagues." Sarek would eventually follow in his footsteps and become Vulcan Ambassador to the United Federation of Planets, located on Earth). He was told to return to Earth and begin negotiating a treaty between the two worlds. Vulcan would, in the meantime, prepare a follow-up survey mission to assist him.

Solkar, looking for a liaison to the Earth's governments, thought immediately of Cochrane. He returned to Montana and asked Cochrane for his assistance to begin a dialogue with the governments of the world. Although Cochrane didn't want to get involved, Solkar persisted.

"Logic suggested," Solkar wrote to his superiors, "that Cochrane's reluctance to assume the post as spokesperson for his species would help to guarantee he wouldn't be serving his own ambitions." Cochrane relented, and took Solkar to San Francisco.

The diplomats who were permanently stationed in the city to enforce the peace treaty that ended WWIII were already aware of the aliens who had landed in Montana. Given the years of conflict on Earth, they fully expected that the first contact was a prelude to an alien invasion.

Matthew Root, a diplomat from the European Hegemony, the government of the European continent, was in San Francisco when radar detected the alien ship approaching the Presidio. He later wrote in a letter to his wife: "We thought 'this is it,' but everyone was too afraid to call in for help. We'd all seen the ship take off from Montana, and since then no military wanted to be the aliens' target. So when they landed on the green lawn, we simply opened our hands and hoped they were peaceful."

Solkar and the Humans immediately began negotiating a treaty. At the same time as he reached out diplomatically, Solkar also covertly supervised survey missions that were gathering as much information as they could on the state of Earth. His surveys found that although Earth was in a relative state of peace, the continued existence of hunger, disease, and pestilence created a looming threat of war all over the planet. And

ABOVE: A Katric Arc, where Vulcans store the *Katra* (living spirit) of their honored dead. This one purportedly held Surak's.

now that the Humans had warp drive, they had the means to spread their gift for destruction to the rest of the galaxy.

Solkar produced a comprehensive 7,000-page report; its conclusion implied a direct threat to Vulcan interests, and an unusual admission that remained confidential for centuries. His final line read, "The Human race is in many ways reminiscent of pre-reformation Vulcan; left unchecked, it will undoubtedly move out into space and gain access to technological tools that will a) lead to their own self-destruction, and/or b) increase the emotional savagery already prevalent in this section of the Galaxy."

Unknown to the population of Earth, the Vulcan Science Council and the High Command immediately placed the Sol system under Vulcan stewardship. Historians would mark this decision as the seminal moment when Vulcan "logic" became justification for an increasingly colonial agenda that slowly led the culture away from the teachings of Surak. But it also had many positive effects: the Vulcans were technologically dominant in the Alpha Quadrant, so their chief rivals, the Klingons and the Andorians—who certainly would have been more exploitative of the primitive Humans—stayed clear. And it protected Earth from itself, allowing time for the Humans' culture to catch up with their technology.

As Solkar negotiated with the Humans, he made logical assumptions about his leverage. "The primitive barbarity of the Humans made it inevitable that they would see the Vulcans as a chance to advance technologically," he wrote in his report, "so we can use this enticement to help guide Earth to a more peaceful society."

The High Command offered a limited form of trade and controlled access to advanced technology, medicine, subspace radio, and information about the nearby galaxy. But Solkar refused to negotiate with individual nations. "If the Earthlings do not find a solution to negotiate with one voice," Solkar wrote in his study, "nationalistic competitions will immediately reignite."

Though World War III had already put Earth on the slow road to unification, the enticement of advanced technology was a major tipping point, and within a year the nations had established the Trade Council of Earth. Though in no way even close to a world government, the Trade Council established one voice in their dealings with the Vulcans—and an equitable system to share any knowledge that was gained in that relationship.

During this period, Zefram Cochrane saw a marked increase in his own personal influence. "The Vulcans had all this information about the nearby planets and all they had to offer," Cochrane wrote in his autobiography, "but they weren't going to take us there. So the only way to get to these new worlds was my engine." The companies and nations of Earth started commissioning ships.

With an influx of capital, Cochrane thought he would finally be able to indulge in pure research. But that was not to be. "I went right from being an underground inventor to a major industrialist. I never got to be just a scientist." Still, he said, "I took a lot of pride watching my engine being mass-produced and put in a variety of ships."

Meanwhile, the Trade Council of Earth saw that the resources that would help solve the problems of their planet—among them dilithium, anti-radiation medications, and terraforming technology that would help revive a

INTERSTELLAR COMMERCE ACT OF 2068

The Governments of the nations of Earth have resolved to:

- **STRENGTHEN** the bonds of friendship and cooperation among their nations;
- **CONTRIBUTE** to the harmonious development and expansion of intergalactic trade and provide a catalyst to broader intergalactic cooperation;
- **ESTABLISH** clear and mutually advantageous rules governing trade with other worlds;
- **ENHANCE** the competitiveness in intergalactic markets;
- **FOSTER** creativity and innovation;
- **CREATE** new employment opportunities and improve working conditions and living standards in their respective nations;
- **PRESERVE** their flexibility to safeguard the welfare of the people of Earth;
- **PROMOTE** sustainable development;
- **PROTECT**, enhance, and enforce basic workers' rights;

Have agreed that, to further these goals, to **ESTABLISH, ON THIS DAY**, July 2, 2068, the **TRADE COUNCIL OF EARTH**.

THE OBJECTIVES of the **TRADE COUNCIL**, as elaborated more specifically through its principles and rules, are to:

Eliminate barriers to trade in, and facilitate the movement of, goods and services between Earth and other planets;

Increase substantially the investment opportunities in the territories of the nations of Earth, and their territories in the solar system;

Provide adequate and effective protection and enforcement of intellectual property rights in each nation's territory;

Create effective procedures for the implementation and application of this Agreement, for its joint administration and for the resolution of disputes; and

Establish a framework for further planetary cooperation to expand and enhance the benefits of this Agreement.

decimated world—were now within reach, but the Vulcans made it clear they weren't going to hand them to Earth. This had a further unifying effect on Humanity, as the nations saw that they had no choice but to work together to find their way out into the Milky Way. Wanting results as fast as possible, the Trade Council approved a grand project that they hoped would help to relieve the pressures on what was still a dying Earth: the Great Experiment.

THE GREAT EXPERIMENT

Only a few years after Cochrane's warp flight, the government of the Americas, in an attempt to be the first to get a foothold in space, took advantage of the new warp engine and built a spaceship christened the *S.S. Valiant*. The project was rushed, and its crew of twenty-five was lost in space within a few years of its launch in 2065. (Their fate would not be discovered for another two centuries.)

The *Valiant* crew's one major discovery before it was lost was a habitable planet with no intelligent life, discovered near the star 61 Cygni A, about eleven light-years away from Earth. This fired up the imagination of one woman, Davida Rossi, chief minister of the Trade Council of Earth. "This," she said in an oral history created during the project, "is what the people need. A new world to replace the old one."

ABOVE: The original Utopia Planitia shipyard on the surface of Mars, circa 2090. **OPPOSITE:** The Vulcan requirement that Earth "trade with one voice" forced the nations of Earth to hammer out an agreement by which to do that. Hence, the Interstellar Commerce Act to establish the Trade Council of Earth.

Rossi immediately launched what she dubbed the Great Experiment. Rossi negotiated protocols with the Trade Council for the first worldwide space program, requiring participation of every nation to complete it. This was a step up from the initial trade agreements, because it required that the nations produce and provide, and not just receive. The project inspired some significant achievements: the New Berlin colony was established on Earth's moon and, a few years after that, the Utopia Planitia base on Mars.

These outposts of Humanity initially had a singular purpose: to provide construction and supply bases for an interstellar ship to colonize the newly discovered planet. Simultaneously, an international team of scientists was commissioned to design a colony ship, and manufacturers were contracted to build it. Mining colonies were set up in the asteroid belt to provide the necessary resources for construction.

It was an unbelievable undertaking, unlike anything in Earth's history, and three years after the discovery of the planet, the ship was complete: the *S.S. Conestoga*, named for the wagons used by settlers in the nineteenth-century American West. The ship would carry 200 colonists in suspended animation to this new planet, named Terra Nova—literally "New Earth."

Chosen for command of the mission was Captain Andrew Paul Mitchell, a genuine war hero. At the age of twenty-one, Mitchell had graduated from the last class of the Air Force Academy. "I came out of an Air Force family," Mitchell said in an interview just before the launch, "and my parents remembered what it was like to live in a free America." As an adult, Mitchell bristled at the authoritarianism that had taken over his country, and eventually he became part of the underground, playing a crucial role in overthrowing Colonel Green's government.

Mitchell was believed to be a perfect choice for the mission. "He was a bold, brave, uncompromising leader," Rossi

BELOW: Davida Rossi and Andrew Paul Mitchell with two Vulcan advisers in front of the "Great Experiment," the *Conestoga*.

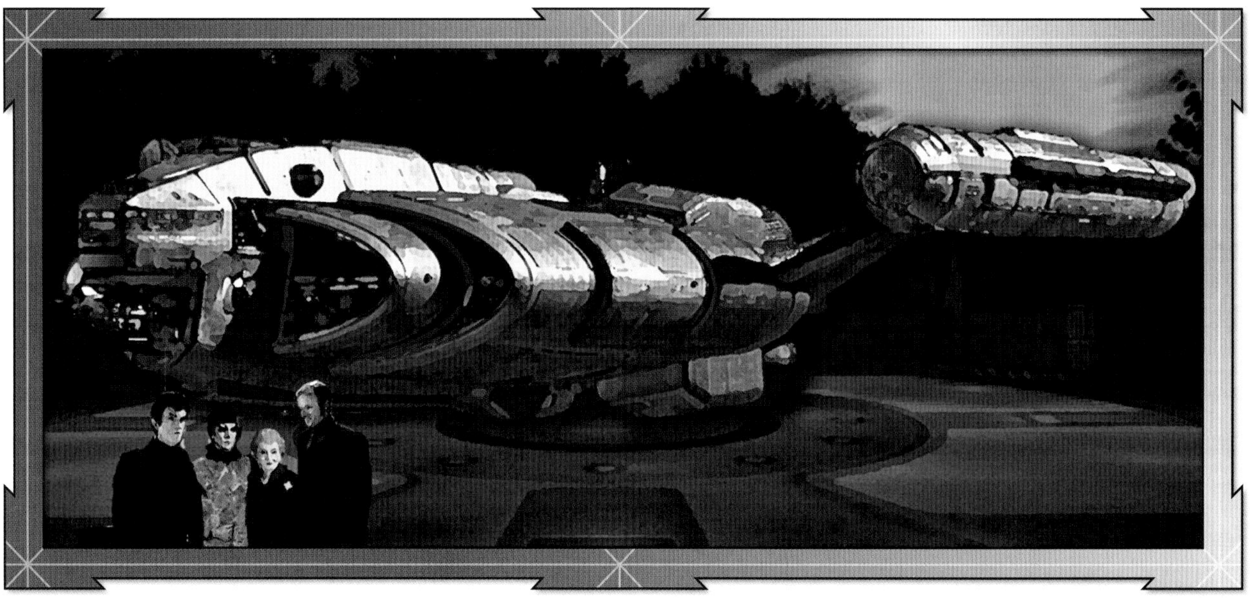

wrote. "He had lost his entire family in the war, leaving him with no ties to Earth. I thought he was perfect, but ironically it was these qualities that would make me regret my choice."

It took nine years for *Conestoga* to reach the new world. Once there and awakened, Mitchell and the rest of the colonists—also chosen for their lack of ties to Earth—happily cannibalized the ship to build their colony. There was no going home. When the first transmissions from the new colony were received, the world celebrated. And Minister Rossi immediately implemented plans to repeat her success. Rossi communicated to Mitchell that a second ship was already being built, and a new group of colonists being selected.

But the trip to Terra Nova was an arduous one, and survival on the planet was far from easy. The colonists, led by Mitchell, felt that their accomplishments were all their own. They didn't want to be dictated to by Earth. "I couldn't believe it," Rossi said. "Mitchell told me they didn't want the new colonists, that they wouldn't accept them."

Rossi, communicating with Mitchell via subspace, grew resentful of his attitude. "I lost my temper," Rossi said. "I told Mitchell he wouldn't even be there if it wasn't for me. And each time we spoke, it got worse." Finally Terra Nova ceased to respond. Rossi, assuming Mitchell was purposely cutting off communication, continued to try to contact the colony, even apologized, but with no success.

"It had gotten so heated between us," Rossi said, "that I worried a second colony ship might actually be attacked. So I canceled the project."

The fact that the colony had been decimated by an asteroid impact would not be discovered until decades after Rossi's death. As a result, she took unnecessary responsibility for what she considered her greatest failure. Yet the endeavor ended up a watershed moment, requiring such a level of resources and labor, and holding so much promise for so many people that it solidified the working relationships between the nations of Earth. Twenty years later, in 2099, a United Earth Government was founded, and its Constitution was built on Rossi's protocols for international cooperation to build the *Conestoga*.

SLOW AND STEADY

Despite its long-term influence, at the time the Terra Nova colony went silent, the project was considered an epic disaster. The experience convinced Earth to refocus. Another plan, developed during the construction of the *Conestoga* but put on the back burner, was now brought to the forefront.

"The biggest problem Humans face in traveling to the stars," Cochrane said later in life to one of his many biographers, "was that dilithium was not native to Earth. If it had been, we wouldn't have needed the Vulcans at all."

The Vulcans had been willing to provide only a small continuing supply, so if Humanity was ever going to independently explore the stars, Earth had to develop its own pipeline. This created a dilemma: In order to explore the stars, Humans needed dilithium, but in order to acquire it, they needed to explore the stars. The only way to do that was to trade. Thus, the Earth Cargo Service (E.C.S.) was established.

The infrastructure developed for the building of the *Conestoga* was immediately turned over to the E.C.S. There were still enough resources on the moon, Mars, and the mining colonies of the asteroid belt to build more interstellar ships. And there were resources unique to the Sol system so that the traders had something to trade. With a small supply of dilithium, and a new engine designed by Cochrane himself that could reach Warp 1.8, the first wave of cargo freighters—the J class and later the Y class—were built, loaded, and launched.

Because these new ships would carry cargo that had to be protected and monitored, and enter trade routes where they would encounter other ships, the crew could not be in suspended animation. Though it was faster than Humans had ever traveled before, the years involved in reaching other inhabited solar systems required that the trading ships be crewed by people willing to spend the greater chunk of their lives in space.

"Fortunately for the space program," Davida Rossi said later, "Earth was still pretty terrible. We thought we would have trouble getting volunteers but it was the opposite. There were hundreds of people for whom Earth held no attraction." As a result, generations of Human children would be born and raised between the stars. Nicknamed "Boomers," their life-long experiences in interstellar space travel would eventually become vital to the initial successes of the future Starfleet. They were the first Human ambassadors to other worlds, bringing the wonders of their neighbors in the nearby galaxy home to Earth.

The trade routes eventually opened up; the ships returned to Earth from the Vega Colony, the moons of Tenebia, and Trilias Prime with not only dilithium, but other goods and information from species who, unlike the Vulcans, were very willing to trade with Earth.

It took a long time, but as a result of this period of trade, Humans also learned ways to revitalize their planet. The irradiated soil was healed and rejuvenated with anti-radiation treatments. Food production began again, this time without the divisions and competitions caused by separate governments, but rather with the idea of feeding everybody. Space industry employed first hundreds of thousands and then millions. Education became a requirement to survive in the new age, and the trade council helped re-establish schools and universities throughout the world. Self-enrichment and individual achievement became the goals of the Human race. Earth was entering a golden age.

WARP 5!

In 2101, Cochrane, looking for peace from his fame on Earth, led an expedition to terraform a colony in the nearby star system of Alpha Centauri. Because of the attention Cochrane brought to this project, the Proxima Centauri colony thrived and would eventually become a civilization in its own right.

In 2121, Cochrane returned to Earth. Although he was known to say that he was old at thirty (and years of alcohol abuse and exposure to radiation indeed made him look like a man of sixty when the Vulcans arrived on Earth), at ninety, Zefram Cochrane was indeed actually getting old. The advances in medicine developed as a result of interstellar trade extended his life, but too much damage had been done early on. He was a wealthy, powerful, influential man who had lived to see his world almost destroyed, then reborn into a paradise. Yet he was frustrated. "I got to help build Proxima, but I really wanted to see the Galaxy," Cochrane said. "It was all out there, but I would never get to it." Like many men of his time, he had begun to blame the Vulcans. "They had ships that could travel at Warp 5," he said, "and we still hadn't broken Warp 2." Cochrane decided his last living act would change that.

He found his answer in the graduate work of a young engineer named Henry Archer, then an associate professor in engineering at the State University of New York at Albany. Archer's PhD dissertation was a workable design for a Warp 5 engine.

"I'm reading this thing," Cochrane said, "and I can't believe it. This kid had pulled together every scrap of information we'd learned about traveling faster than light, and that was only in the first third. He then laid out a plan." Archer laid out the steps of developing the infrastructure necessary to invent the myriad new technologies necessary to build this engine.

"It was brilliant," wrote Cochrane. "He covered everything. It helped me see that my engineers and I had wanted to change things overnight, which is why we couldn't crack it. I had to accept that this wasn't going to happen in my lifetime. But it was going to happen." Cochrane acted immediately.

According to an interview with Henry Archer published in the *Albany Times-Union* newspaper, Cochrane simply showed up without announcement at Archer's modest home near the university. When Archer's eight-year-old son Jonathan answered the door, Cochrane smiled and asked if his father was at home. The young Archer, who had been instructed to expect a repairperson, said his dad wasn't home and asked Cochrane if he was going to fix the refrigerator. Cochrane didn't skip a beat, saying, "I'll give it a shot."

"When I came home," Henry Archer related in the interview, "I walked into the kitchen to find my son and the world's most famous man working on the innards of the ice maker. Cochrane turned to me and said, 'Hi, when I'm done with this, I want to talk to you about building your engine.'"

Once Henry Archer was on board, Cochrane put him in charge of a development team that immediately began

ABOVE: Henry Archer and his eight-year-old son Jonathan.

Day 3 - In some ways, this is easier than I thought. No one shows the least bit of curiosity about me. Yesterday, I found some place to live, a little room and bath over this old woman's house. She didn't ask to see any identity papers, just accepted who I said I was. No suspicion, no guarantees, just trusting that I was being honest. Then I walked into the High Command today and said I wanted to work as a janitor. No one even questioned it. The forged papers I had were very superficially examined, then they told me I could start tomorrow. Had a lot of trouble not looking surprised.

Day 41 - It's generally so serene here, it starts to affect you; it makes it mostly easy to control my emotions in public, but then something unexpected happens and it's all I can do to keep from shouting... Today on the street a vehicle lost control, slammed into this little kid, probably 7 years old, mother is standing there... mother checks on the son, who isn't moving, then the mother goes over to the driver and asks if he's injured. No reaction from anyone, and the kid is just lying there dead in the road. Had to leave. I got back to my room, I thought, how could she not react? But she didn't seem in pain, it seemed to spare her pain. But there had to be pain... I don't get it.

Day 392 - I was cleaning a computer monitoring room today. The technician on duty, just like every day, left to use the bathroom at approximately the same time after his mid-afternoon meal. I had gathered security codes, and knew that I would have enough time to gain access to the files I was interested in. After the technician left, however, I had second thoughts. What was the logic in it? If I discovered that the Vulcans indeed did have ulterior motives, what action would I take? I would tell my government. What would they do? Earth's entire military forces would be completely outmatched by even one Vulcan battleship. There was no logic to my mission. It doesn't make sense. Then the computer technician returned from the bathroom. Maybe I will try tomorrow.

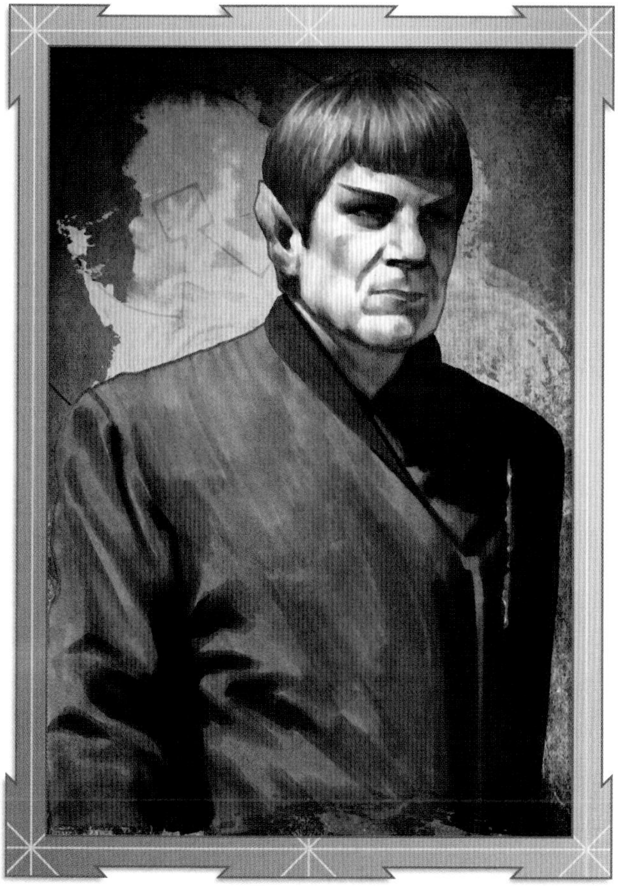

crunching the numbers to bring Archer's plan to fruition. They estimated the engine would take twenty-five years to build. Cochrane then brought the plan to the United Earth Government, and, as he predicted, they immediately supported it. "They weren't going to say no to me," he said.

The twenty-five-year plan commenced with a slow but steady stream of help from the Vulcans. But this changed when the Vulcan High Command became aware of Cochrane's plan, the substance of which was a cause of great concern.

Minister V'Las, a rising star in the High Command, made a compelling case supported by logical arguments that they were facing a very different problem than the one they faced when they discovered Earth. "When we first came upon them," V'Las said in a secret speech to the High Command, "we were preventing a savage race from unnaturally launching themselves to the center of galactic affairs. Now we are faced with the possibilities that the Earthlings will be adversaries."

Indeed, in less than one hundred years, the Human race had solved the problems that took 1,500 years for Vulcan to conquer. "If Earth succeeds in outpacing Vulcan technologically," V'Las continued, "we might find ourselves dominated by an inferior race." This argument found adherents; although Vulcans do their best to bury it, they can feel fear.

Solkar, still the ambassador to Earth, did not agree with V'Las's assessment. He found the slow and steady progress

---

LEFT: Minister V'Las, a rising star in the Vulcan High Command, who would eventually become its administrator. **OPPOSITE:** Zebulon Carter was a twenty-first-century Earthling who pulled off one of the greatest feats in the history of spycraft: he passed himself off as a Vulcan. In 2073, the American government, worried that the Vulcans had secret plans for conquest over Earth, had Carter undergo surgery; he was given passage on the *E.C.S. North Star*, on a trade route that took it to Vulcan. Once on the planet, Carter slipped off the ship and began his life as a Vulcan. His mission was to discover what ulterior motives the Vulcans had. He never reported back. His journal was found on Vulcan in 2252 and returned to Earth. These are selected passages from his journal, which indicate he found employment as a janitor in the High Command. The passages suggest that Carter may have "gone native," and the journal appears a microcosm for the civilizing effect the Vulcans had on the Human race in general.

the Humans were making agreeable and appropriate, and thought there was no need to change policy, but the High Command overruled him. They voted on a plan to slow down to a trickle any further help to the Humans on their Warp 5 project, but to do so without seriously jeopardizing Human-Vulcan relations. It was a delicate line to walk, and the High Command decided to replace Solkar with a new ambassador to Earth to oversee this change in policy.

The choice was a member of the Vulcan Diplomatic Corps named Soval. He was specifically chosen because he had begun his career in military intelligence, serving as part of the occupation force on Weytahn, a planetoid on the border between the Andorian and Vulcan systems that was the source of a long dispute. The Andorians had terraformed and colonized Weytahn, and the Vulcans tried to occupy it due to concerns that it was a secret base for a planned military action against them. Soval became an authority on the Andorians and had a hand in the territorial compromise that brought peace to Weytahn. When he transferred to the diplomatic corps, he became a vital resource in Vulcan dealings with Andoria.

When V'Las approached Soval about the assignment to Earth, he drew connections between the violent, arrogant Andorians and the citizens of Earth. "Minister V'Las drew many parallels between Andoria and Earth," Soval wrote to his wife, informing her of his occupation change. "I have seen many comrades die at the hands of the Andorians. It is agreeable to me that I might help prevent another species from having that kind of destructive influence in the galaxy."

By the time Soval made it to Earth, however, Cochrane had already managed to get his project under way. Although the Warp 5 project would take five years longer than the original twenty-five-year plan had predicted, the change in Vulcan policy would not prevent its completion. Within two years of meeting Henry Archer, the ground was broken on the Warp 5 complex—on the same site as the missile complex where the *Phoenix* was built. The building would eventually house 20,000 employees—all working on this one massive undertaking.

But, as Cochrane predicted, he did not see his dream realized. The stress of the undertaking had further deteriorated his health. He believed his time had come, and did not seek the aid of doctors. Instead, one night, he took a small warp ship his company had designed (but never marketed) and left Earth, never to be seen again. Suddenly, the engine that would put Humankind in the center of the Galaxy was in the hands of a young academic, and, eventually, the academic's son—the boy who told Zefram Cochrane to fix the refrigerator.

OPPOSITE: The opening page of the treaty between Vulcan and Earth. Although the preamble seems to imply two parties on an equal footing, the key phrase "counsel on the internal affairs of the receiving party" guaranteed that Vulcan would have influence over Earth's internal affairs.

TRADE AGREEMENT

BETWEEN THE PEOPLES OF

EARTH AND VULCAN

The Vulcan High Command and the Trade Council of Earth, hereinafter referred to as the Parties, working to forge a strategic relationship based on mutual trust, openness, predictability, and cooperation between their two worlds,

Understanding that both worlds will gain from the mutual exchange of knowledge, but recognizing the inherent risks of that exchange,

Recognizing terms and conditions need to be codified where one of the Parties provides information (including but not limited to an innovation, advancement, or development in an area of knowledge) to the other Party,

Also recognizing the necessity that the receiving Party of information as defined in the previous paragraph needs regulation by the delivering Party, up to and including counsel on the internal affairs of the receiving Party,

Guided by the principle of mutual growth and convinced that the limits and obligations set forth in this Treaty will enhance the stability of the relationship between both Parties,

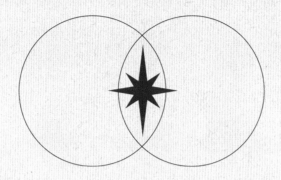

Welcoming the implementation of the Trade Agreement between the Vulcan High Command and the Trade Council of Earth on December 13, 2073.

CHAPTER I

FIRST STEPS

2120–2155

"Up until about a hundred years ago . . . there was one question that burned in every Human: 'Are we alone?' Our generation is privileged to know the answer to that question."

—Jonathan Archer, speech to the delegates of the Coalition of Planets, 2154

OPPOSITE: Nathan Samuels speaking at the first meeting of what would become the Coalition of Planets.

On Earth, the decades following the groundbreaking on the Warp 5 project would be prosperous and relatively uneventful. Humanity's initial rush of desire to get into space went largely unfulfilled; though ships populated by families plied the trade routes and a few other Humans traded places with friendly alien species through exchange programs, such as the Inter-Species Medical Exchange, the limits that technology placed on space exploration kept most Humans at home.

But the Warp 5 engine was set to change all that. It was ironic, then, that just a few weeks from the scheduled launch of the ship that was to open up the Galaxy, an unforeseen incident put Earth at the center of interstellar affairs. It led to a completely unexpected chain of events that would—over the course of only a few years—conclude with Humanity itself founding the Coalition of Planets, the forerunner of the Federation.

BROKEN BOW

As he would relate in countless interviews with media outlets, Richard Moore did not expect to make history as he sat at his kitchen table the morning of April 1, 2151, eating his breakfast of biscuits and gravy. "I'm a corn farmer," he said, "the only thing on my mind was corn."

His breakfast was suddenly interrupted by the sound of a crash. "I ran outside, saw the smoke and these flashes in the distance, and I think, 'I'm bein' invaded.'" Though it had been almost a century since alien beings first made contact with Earth, Moore was among the great majority of Humans who had never seen one in person. He had more than once thought about joining Terra Prime, a group that advocated an alien-free Earth, but he didn't think of himself as being political. His only worry that morning was his family farm. "I got my plasma rifle. Those monsters weren't goin' to use their brain-sucking weapons on me and take my land."

Moore related that he was about fifty feet away when the farm's methane storage tank exploded. When he reached the rubble, there it was. "It was a monster . . . " he said, "but it also kinda looked like a guy. It had long hair and these weird ridges on its forehead, and it shouted at me. I couldn't understand what in heck it was saying, but I could tell it was angry."

Moore tried to warn it off, but the creature kept coming, so Moore aimed his rifle and fired. "First time I ever shot anything besides crows or rats," Moore said. The plasma bolt hit the alien dead in the chest, and it flew back into the corn stalks. Thus, a Human encountered a Klingon for the first time. It was not unlike the many future engagements the two species would have.

The Klingon's name was Klaang, and he was a member of a species considered one of the most dangerous in the Alpha Quadrant. The Klingons referred to themselves as a "warrior race," and, like Surak did for the Vulcans, one Klingon had set the tone for their philosophy. An ancient warrior, Kahless, united a disparate people by emphasizing a unique code of honor, including a complex mythology surrounding war and death.

Kahless's teachings created a very unified but aggressive society that, when it finally made it into space, saw other races as inferior. This was a convenient philosophy because the Klingon Empire required resources to expand. At the time of Klaang's crash, the Klingons were much further advanced technologically than Humanity. Had it not been for the Vulcan stewardship, Earth quickly would have been added to the Empire.

Species like the Klingons were one of many reasons Vulcan Ambassador Soval had kept a strong hand in Human affairs, holding them back from fully becoming part of the galactic community for as long as he could. "It was known to anyone with even a superficial knowledge of the Klingons," Soval said, in his report to his superiors about the encounter, "that they didn't just accept death, but glorified it, especially when that Klingon had died doing his duty." Conversely, being spared by an enemy was dishonorable.

When Klaang crashed in Moore's cornfield, he had been carrying secret information back to the High Council, the Klingons' ruling body. (The information, it would turn out, proved that outsiders were fomenting a civil war within the Empire.) Though Klaang's wounds were treatable, Soval and the Vulcans knew enough about Klingon culture to understand that it would be better to let him die and take his body back to Qo'noS (pronounced "Kronos"), the Klingon Homeworld, as the Empire demanded.

"If this situation is mishandled," Soval said to his superiors, "Humans and Klingons could be in conflict for generations." Soval strongly suggested to the United Earth Government that the Vulcans take over the disposition of Klaang's body. Soval also hoped that his management of the situation with Klaang would provide him another opportunity to hold Humans back a little longer (the slowing of the Vulcan's initial help had only managed to extend the Warp 5 project for an extra five years). He was trying to protect them from a race of people that he felt they weren't ready to understand. But his warnings went unheeded; the Humans had grown impatient and Vulcan's influence was waning. Humanity could now do what it wanted; it was about to have its own Warp 5 ship.

LEFT: Traditional Klingon clothing and weaponry, circa 2150.

THE NX PROJECT AND STARFLEET COMMAND

"In its infancy, the Warp 5 project faced two almost-crushing setbacks," wrote Kotaro Tasaki, the director of the project for most of its thirty years. "When Cochrane disappeared," Tasaki said in the official history of the project, "I figured we were done, but Henry said we could continue. So we did, and then Henry got sick."

In the first year of the project, Archer developed Clarke's disease, a degenerative condition of the brain. Archer deteriorated into hallucinations quickly and died within a few years of being diagnosed.

"I was left in charge," Tasaki said. "I didn't think I was up to it, and I wanted to just go home. I was nothing compared to these great men. But they had left detailed plans, and I felt I couldn't let them down."

Along with the development of the technologies to build the engine and the first Warp 5 ship (called the NX program), the project's mission also included the training of crews to pilot the ship. Cochrane and Archer's plan was to build a succession of engines, testing them in actual space travel. The United Earth Government would then have the ability to commission ships using these intermediate engines, and the data collected from the practical application of these experimental engines would then be fed back into the program for the next step. United Earth would be dependent on the program to provide personnel to operate the ships, and Cochrane and Archer had planned to formalize the crews under a military structure.

Thus, Starfleet Command was born. It was an institution that would oversee Humankind's exploration of the Galaxy. But Starfleet was unlike previous military organizations. Given the limited amount of space aboard starships, the crews would need to have overlapping areas of knowledge in order to provide the necessary support in critical situations.

"A crew member's area of knowledge," Henry Archer wrote in his detailed explanation of Starfleet, "could not begin and end with how to fire a gun." As a result, Starfleet crew members were given exceptional educations. This had the unintended consequence that the people on the ships of Earth had an unusual intellectual openness, which was fortunate given what was to become the first mission

LEFT: The main hall of the Klingon High Council on Qo'noS. **OPPOSITE:** The final approved design of the first Warp 5 starship, the *Enterprise* NX-01.

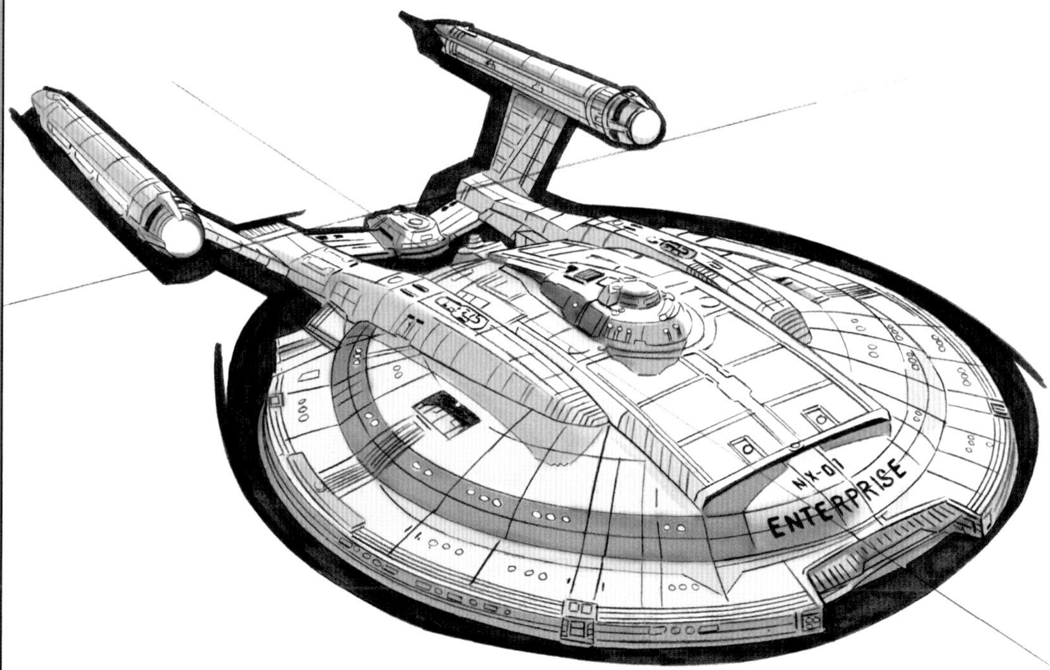

APPROVED JUNE 1, 2140

MAXWELL FORREST

MEMORY ALPHA LCARS HARD COPY EXTRACT

ORIGINAL SOURCE: UNITED EARTH INFORMATION SERVICE	18.6.2118

MOLECULAR TRANSPORT EXPERIMENT A SUCCESS!

Organic material disappears—then reappears—in a new location.

By Talia Rose Felson

CHICAGO, IL—The banana disappeared; it then reappeared twenty feet away.

This was the organic material physicist/engineer Emory Erickson decided to use to demonstrate his molecular transportation device, an invention that—if practical—will have applications in a wide variety of fields. On hand for the demonstration were reporters, scientists, engineers, as well as Erickson's close friend, Zefram Cochrane.

"I've sent some rocks through before," Erickson said. "Now I wanted something alive."

Once the banana reappeared, Erickson decided to conduct a test to see if it was intact. So he ate it. "I think it worked," he said, mouth full of banana.

Erickson's device consists of two large chambers, each connected to a computer and a power source, but in no way connected to each other. "The object that is going to be beamed is scanned on the quantum level," Erickson explained in a matter-of-fact tone that belies the device's revolutionary nature. "It makes a map of the object's physical structure, and breaks it down into a stream of subatomic particles, which is sent over subspace to its destination."

There's a control station, and when the device is operated, this process allows the human eye to watch the matter broken down in the subatomic particles, which then reassemble in the other chamber. "The potential isn't just for travel from one point on Earth to another without a vehicle," Erickson said, "It holds the distinct possibility to leave Earth without a spaceship."

"He's trying to put me out of business," joked Cochrane.

Erickson, forty-two, has been working on the device for fifteen years, since he was a graduate student at the New University of Chicago. There, he received the Jesse and Hilde Cochrane Fellowship, personally funded by Zefram Cochrane, in honor of his parents. During Erickson's research, Cochrane took an interest in the work, and the two men became acquainted. When it came time to build the practical device, the world's most well known inventor was there to lend a financial hand.

"Emory is a true visionary," Cochrane said. "It was my pleasure to help. But he would've gotten here without me."

After the successful test, Cochrane and Erickson joked about its future. "When's that thing going to be ready for people?" Cochrane teased.

"Get on in there," Erickson said, indicating the chamber. "We'll give it a whirl. It's about time you get famous for something else."

of the first Warp 5 ship, the *Enterprise* NX-01. Including its commander Jonathan Archer.

JONATHAN ARCHER

There were plenty of circumstances in his life that led Jonathan Archer into space. His father, Henry Archer, designed warp engines, and as a child Jonathan had met Zefram Cochrane, the world's most famous astronaut, several times. And because of his father's crucial role in the development of warp technology, young Jonathan developed many close relationships with the premier scientists of the day, including Emory Erickson, who would invent the first molecular transporter. All of these factors may have opened his mind to the idea of scientific exploration, but Archer's many biographers agree that the tipping point was the death of his father: determination to connect with his lost parent drove Archer's achievements.

Emory Erickson's daughter, in a book she wrote about her father, relayed a comment the revered scientist made about Archer. "Dad said Jonathan didn't just want to be on the first ship with his father's engine; he *needed* to be its captain."

Archer was also driven to prove that Humanity deserved its place in outer space. For many years, as a child and well into adulthood, Archer nursed a grudge against the Vulcans. "If the Vulcans hadn't been so stingy," Archer wrote in a letter to his mother, "Dad might have lived to see his dream come true."

Accepted at Starfleet and the NX program at the age of twenty, Archer proved himself to be a valuable resource. "This kid [Archer] just told me what was wrong with the reactor," wrote Matthew Jefferies, an engineer on the project, in a memo to Archer's superior officer,"and he was right. If he wants to come over to engineering, I'd love to have him."

But Archer wanted to be a pilot, and as the NX test program proceeded, he rose through the ranks, testing engines and test-flying ships, until he was one of the top four choices to command the Warp 5 ship. (The paradoxical nature of the NX program was that because the ship was more advanced than anything previously built, the best choices for the top spot of captain had served most of their duty on Earth or within the solar system.)

Throughout his initial assignments, Archer was known as a by-the-book officer. He changed, however, after an accident with the intermediate engine that was set to break the Warp 2 barrier. The design of Henry Archer's engine was initially blamed for the accident, and the NX program—many years in—was threatened with being sent back to the drawing board. Archer, with the assistance of another pilot, J. G. Robinson, stole a prototype ship and proved that his father's engine design was sound. He also proved he knew how to take initiative.

This incident transformed both his self-image and the impression his superiors had of him, and over time helped create a different officer. "I no longer have concerns about Commander Archer," his superior officer Admiral Maxwell Forrest wrote in his recommendation for Archer's promotion to captain. "He is the best candidate to command *Enterprise*."

OPPOSITE: Emory Erickson owed the success of his invention, the molecular transporter, to many of the scientific breakthroughs that Cochrane made in inventing warp drive. Erickson would face personal tragedy later in his life when he lost his son in a transporter accident.

Although Forrest no longer had concerns, Archer's developing decisiveness worried the Vulcans. Soval openly lobbied for another candidate, Captain Gardner, whom Soval saw as "less impulsive." And Soval believed his concerns were confirmed when Archer's first act as the newly commissioned captain of the *Enterprise* was convincing Admiral Forrest to save Klaang's life and let *Enterprise* return him to his homeworld. This would be the ship's first mission.

Soval, knowing that he was unable to stop the launch of *Enterprise* or its first mission, used his still considerable influence to place one of his subordinates, Subcommander T'Pol, on the ship. "Soval has given me instructions to specifically help temper Archer's impulsiveness," T'Pol wrote in her personal log on her first day on *Enterprise*. "After a few minutes with the captain I have doubts that I will succeed in this endeavor." But she was wrong. T'Pol did in the end play a large role in helping Archer safely return Klaang to the Klingons without triggering an immediate conflict. (Archer's future interactions with the Klingons would not be as "friendly"; more than once he would go up against them, to the point that he was branded a criminal by the Empire.)

This first assignment was considered a wild success, and after returning Klaang to Qo'noS, *Enterprise* continued on its originally planned extended mission. As stated in Cochrane's speech in the breaking of ground for the Warp 5 complex, *Enterprise* would explore strange new worlds and seek out new life and new civilizations.

And because *Enterprise*, to paraphrase Cochrane, was going where no Human had gone before, necessity became

LEFT: Soval, Vulcan ambassador to Earth.

the mother of invention. Many of the devices and protocols that would become commonplace on ships of the Starfleet were developed on this first voyage. It was the first time that hand phasers (in the form of early phase pistols) were used by a starship crew, considered to be a more humane weapon because it introduced the "stun" setting. The ship's communications officer, faced with the nearly impossible task of translating a vast number of new languages, developed her own version of what would become the universal translator. The tactical officer, finding he had to ready the ship for more battles than anyone expected, refined the defensive systems and created a protocol that would evolve into the starship color alert system. But perhaps the greatest template the first *Enterprise* created was exemplified by Archer himself. From that first mission of the first starship, it became abundantly clear that the man or woman who would have the job of captain could not just be an explorer.

"I learned very quickly," Archer said late in life in a speech to a graduating class at Starfleet Academy, "that I

RIGHT: Sub-commander T'Pol, the first Vulcan to serve on a Starfleet ship. **FOLLOWING SPREAD:** A study by a Federation research subcommittee trying to determine the roots of the conflict between Klingons and Humans found it traced back to this internal report by the Klingon High Council on the incident involving Klaang's crash on Earth and subsequent return. The report was made public in the Empire, and had far-reaching effects. After the effect of Archer's actions became known, the Federation subcommittee recommended strict guidelines before engaging in first contact with an alien species. Its report would directly lead a few years later to the creation of the Prime Directive.

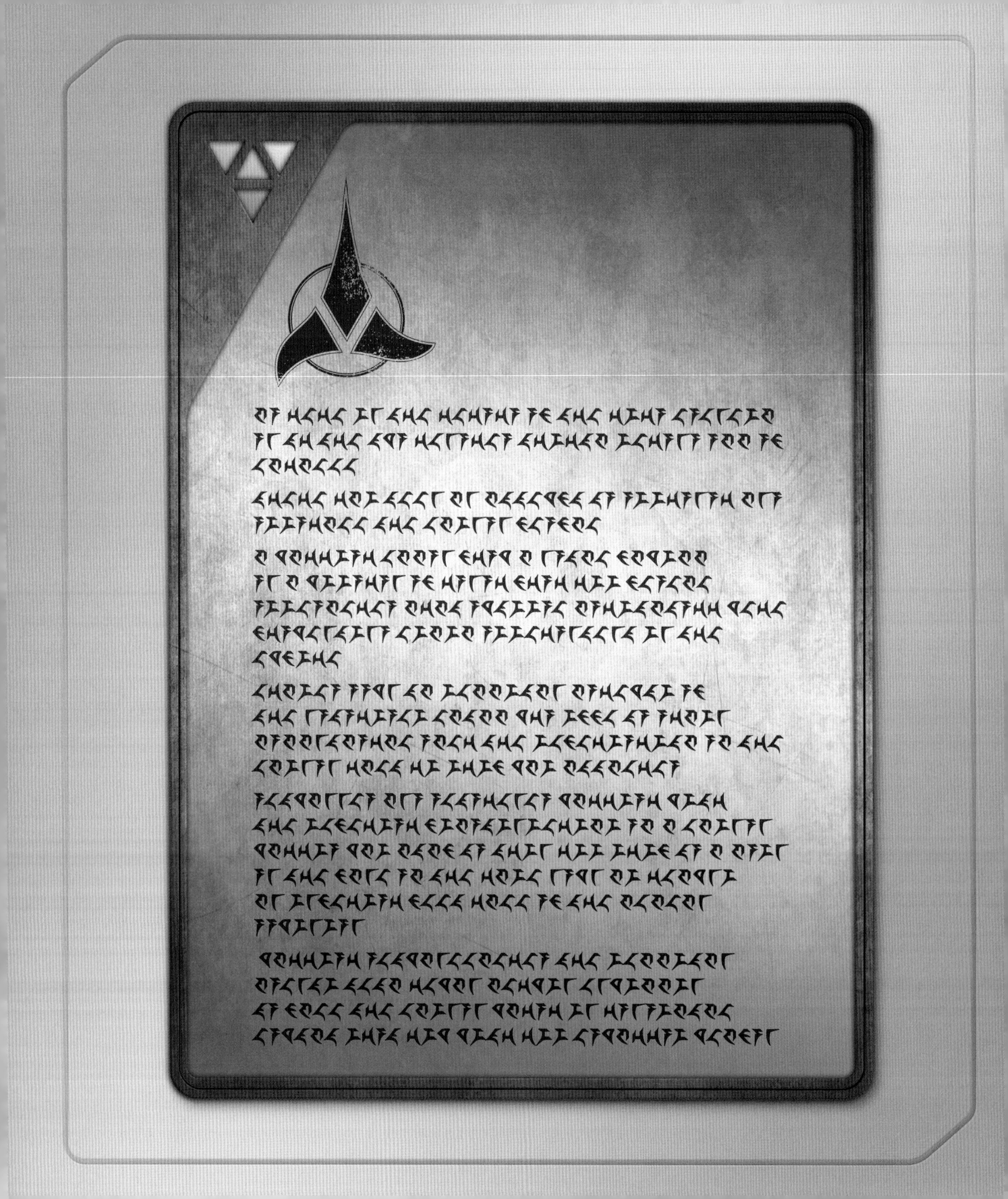

REPORT TO KLINGON HIGH COUNCIL ON ARCHER

TRANSLATED FROM THE KLINGON

Lo! Here is the record of the High Council on this, the two hundred thirty-second day of the six hundred eighty-fifth year of Kahless!

There has been an attempt to dishonor and disgrace the Klingon people! A warrior, Klaang, from a noble family, on a mission of honor for his people, discovered that outside agitators were fomenting civil discontent in the Empire. Chased down by Suliban agents of the notorious Cabal—who seek to gain advantage over the superiority of the Klingon race—his ship was attacked. Outmanned and outgunned, Klaang, with the superior piloting skills of a Klingon warrior, was able to bring his ship to a landing on the planet of the race known as Humans, an inferior puppet race of the Vulcan Dominion. Klaang outmaneuvered the inferior Suliban, but a Human vermin, unwilling to face the Klingon warrior in honorable combat, shot him with his coward's weapon.

Klaang's life should have ended honorably. If the honorable body had been delivered to the High Council, the information that Klaang encoded in his DNA would have made its way to us. But the inferior Humans intervened! They cured his wounds with liquids and powders that are abhorrent to the Klingon warrior! They claim no knowledge of our ways, but this is a lie! What kind of race would save a life of a warrior so clearly superior? So clearly made to conquer them! They have purposely disgraced Klaang and by extension the Klingon people, and have tried to hide behind the weak face of ignorance. The Human race is not to be trusted; they are meddlers and without honor. From this day forward, they shall be considered enemies of the Empire.

And that the Klingon people not be disgraced by these actions of the Humans, the High Council deems that Klaang is now dishonored, his house stripped of its titles and its lands seized. Klaang will spend the remainder of his life on the penal asteroid Rura Penthe. The honor of the Klingon people has been saved!

had to be a police officer, a rescue worker, and, probably most important, a diplomat. I wasn't trained for most of it." Fortunately for Earth, it was Archer's natural, though reluctant, skills in this last area that led several new species to see Humanity as their ally. This would prove especially true with one of the founding members of the Coalition of Planets and, later, the Federation: Andoria.

THE ANDORIAN INCIDENT

Andoria, an icy world in orbit around the gas giant Andor, was an unusual place to find life, and what did survive there was as resilient and formidable as you would expect. Blue-skinned humanoids with antennae whose movement reflected their owners' emotions, the Andorians broke free of the shackles of their cold, barren world and moved out into space in the hope of finding more hospitable land on which to live. What they found very quickly were the Vulcans, who inhabited the neighboring star system. Immediately suspicious of the emotional, arrogant, and aggressive Andorians, the Vulcans sought to contain them. This only made things worse, and for one hundred years the two races maintained a peace that was rarely peaceful. The Vulcans were concerned that the Andorians were planning aggression, and the Andorians were convinced that the Vulcans were continually spying on them as a prelude to invasion.

One of the manifestations of this conflict occurred at the monastery of P'Jem. For centuries this Vulcan sanctuary, on a planet in a system only a few light-years from Andoria, was a place of quiet contemplation where monks practiced the *Kolinahr*, an ancient ritual meant to purge all emotion. The Andorians, however, were convinced that the monastery was a cover for a secret Vulcan spy station, and made several unsuccessful attempts to uncover it. On June 19, 2151, within two months of leaving Earth, *Enterprise* stumbled into the middle of this ongoing conflict.

The *Enterprise* had stopped at P'Jem to learn more about the monastery. "I was merely curious, I'd never seen a Vulcan monastery before," Archer told Forrest later. "I didn't think it was going to get me in so much trouble." He didn't know that a squad from the Andorian Imperial Guard had taken the monks prisoner while searching for proof of the spy station. Upon landing, Archer's party was also taken prisoner.

The Andorian commander, Thy'lek Shran, assuming Archer was in league with the Vulcans, tortured Archer for the information. In an attempt to escape, Archer accidentally uncovered the monastery's secret: beneath it there *was* a surveillance station, which *was*, in fact, spying on the Andorians. He exposed this secret to Shran, who expressed to Archer that the Andorian people were in his debt.

The incident helped Andoria to see Earth as an ally. However, it did little to ease the tensions between Andoria and Vulcan: shortly after finding the surveillance station, the Andorians destroyed it along with the sanctuary. The Vulcans blamed this on Archer's interference.

The troubles between Vulcan and Andor came to a head on the planetoid of Weytahn, and this conflict found Earth—and Archer—playing a decisive role. More than sixty years before, in 2093, the Vulcan High Command had been concerned that the Andorians were planning on using Weytahn to launch an offensive against Vulcan. They demanded an inspection, which the Andorians refused. In response, the High Command annexed the planetoid, renamed it Paan Mokar, and forcibly removed the Andorian colonists, leaving the planet deserted and monitored by an observation satellite.

The loss of this colony was a sore point for the Andorians for many years, and in 2152 they finally took action: The Imperial Guard sent a division to retake the planetoid. The Vulcan High Command retaliated by landing its own troops. Fighting broke out in the abandoned colony, and, with the forces evenly matched, it looked to be a long and bloody conflict. Because of his personal experience surrounding Weytahn/Paan Mokar, Ambassador Soval was dispatched from his posting on Earth to find a diplomatic solution, but with the lack of trust between the two parties, the hopes for peace looked grim.

BELOW: A map of Andoria. The map indicates bodies of water that are in fact always frozen. **FOLLOWING SPREAD:** The initial introduction between Humans and Andorians went from violence to mutual respect in a matter of hours. This is largely considered to have occurred because the first Earthling to meet the Andorians distrusted the Vulcans as much as they did. Commander Shran, who went on to a seat on the Federation Council, wrote about this encounter in his autobiography. It does not completely line up with other non-Andorian accounts. Although Andoria and Vulcan had long been allies at the time that Shran wrote this, it is clear that he had not completely shaken his view of them.

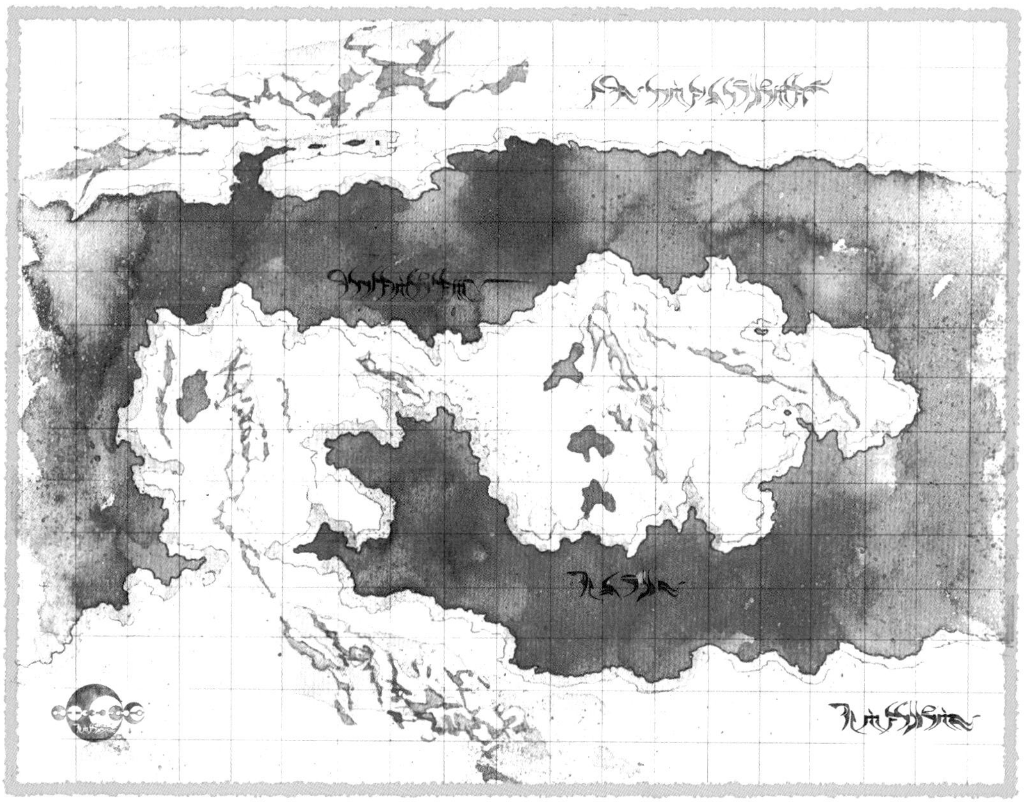

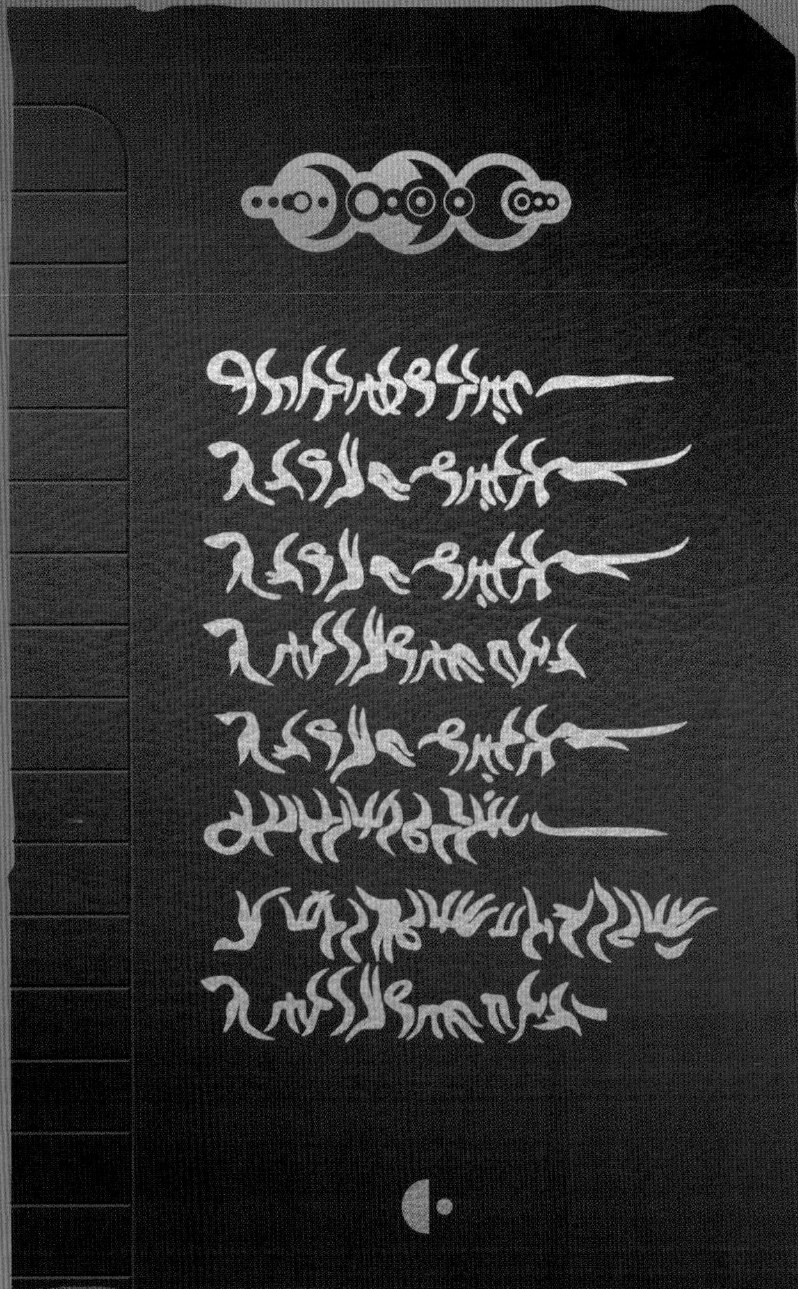

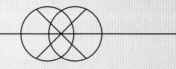

EXCERPT FROM SHRAN'S AUTOBIOGRAPHY

TRANSLATED FROM THE ANDORIAN

Chapter 5: The Pink Skin

I hated Vulcans. When I was given my orders to take my ship to P'Jem, I was filled with sickness. Though they are now our allies, some say our brothers even, it is easy, very easy, to remember a day when they were our adversaries. I didn't trust them; how can you trust a species that is so comfortable with lying? They say they have changed, that the strict teachings of Surak now make them incapable of lying. If I was the soldier I was back then, I would say this too is a lie. But times have changed. I take them at their word.

Then, however, my experience told me the opposite. I had very little proof that the sanctuary on P'Jem was hiding an observation post, that the Vulcans were breaking the treaty and spying on us. But my natural distrust of Vulcans drove away any skepticism I might have had. I arrived on P'Jem and took to beating the Vulcan monks. It is not satisfying beating a Vulcan; they refuse to show pain, to show an emotional response. As a result, you end up dealing out much more abuse than you should, because it appears to be having no effect. The Vulcans wouldn't break, and I was just about to give up when the Pink Skin arrived and we imprisoned him.

He denied any knowledge of the listening post, but I was sure that he was part of the Vulcans' plan to deceive us, that he was working with them, helping them spy on us. So I went to work on him. His response was different than the Vulcans; it was clear I was causing him pain. I continued my efforts, and this only led him to taunt me! I didn't understand this Pink Skin!

There was still no evidence of a listening post; we searched the monastery completely more than once. My men were losing faith in our mission. I expressed unwavering certainty that we would find something, but the truth was that doubt was starting to creep into my thinking, too.

The Pink Skin meanwhile had cleverly called for help from his ship. During the subsequent firefight, the entrance to the listening post was revealed to me. I thanked the Pink Skin. If it had not been for his interference I would never have found it. He was an anomaly to me; he worked with the Vulcans, yet he distrusted them as much as I did, seemed to take pleasure in revealing their secret. And it would turn out our common distrust of the Vulcans would lead me to bring all three worlds together.

There was luck for both sides in the fact that the Andorians had put Shran in charge of the invasion force. "I knew from my experience as a soldier," Shran wrote in his memoirs, "that to win this fight on the battlefield would be too costly." When the Vulcans sent a communiqué to discuss terms for a cease fire, Shran, though suspicious, offered to negotiate through the one "pink skin" he trusted: Jonathan Archer.

"I am not at all comfortable with this prospect," Soval wrote to his superiors, "but it is the only avenue currently being offered. Logic suggests we pursue it." He requested Earth divert *Enterprise*.

Because of the trust Shran placed in Archer, Earth—through Archer's negotiations—was able to bring the two parties to the negotiating table. A lasting, peaceful resolution to the conflict was reached.

This would be the incident that defined Earth's role in the Galaxy—as peacemaker and mediator among the many diverse species and planets. The question as to why Humans are so adept at bringing disparate and often warring species together has long perplexed historians.

The great historian John Gill, in one of his comprehensive surveys, *Small Steps and Giant Leaps: A History of Humankind in the Galaxy*, points to a possibly critical factor: "Each of the other dominant species in the Alpha Quadrant had lived on a united homeworld for centuries before venturing out into the Galaxy; war was a distant memory for them. When conflict presented itself with aliens there were not enough personal memories in the individuals involved for them to instinctively avoid such conflict."

Humans, however, were different. "When we left Earth, war and its horrors were fresh in our collective and individual memories," wrote Gill. "We looked to avoid conflict, to understand who our adversaries were—and who they were not—and to never jump to the conclusion that fighting was the only solution. Even when conflict broke out, Human individuals looked for ways to end it peacefully."

ATTACK ON EARTH

February 3, 2153, became a date much like September 11, 2001, was for the former United States of America—the date of a surprise attack, the reverberations of which would last far beyond the conclusion of the immediate conflict. In the case of 3/2/53 (as it would come to be known), it wasn't just one country attacked, but the entire planet. It was the first alien attack Earth had ever faced. The attacking ship was a one-occupant vessel that came out of a subspace corridor and cut a destructive swath from Florida to Venezuela, then self-destructed. Seven million lives were lost.

The attack stunned, then enraged, the entire Human race. What had been a short and peaceful age of space flight came to an end with a war brought to Earth.

OPPOSITE: Ending a century-long conflict, Vulcan agreed to withdraw from Weytahn and cede ownership of the planetoid to Andoria. This final article lays out the one circumstance under which the treaty will be considered abrogated, and which threatened to send both parties back to war. "It was a bomb that never went off," Jonathan Archer wrote in his autobiography. It is interesting to note that there was only one species listed in Appendix A: Humans.

Article XXII

Andoria agrees that no military installation will be established on the surface of Weytahn.

A) Andoria and Vulcan agree to an annual inspection by a "Third Party Species," drawn from the list agreed to in Appendix A, to determine that Andoria is abiding by Article XXII

1) If "Third Party Species" determines that Andoria has violated Article XXII, this agreement shall be considered null and void.

2) In such event that Andoria is in violation of Article XXII, Andoria shall have eighty-seven hours to dismantle its military installation before Vulcan shall take military action.

This treaty and all related articles and subsections are hereby and irrevocably agreed on this date, the thirteenth day of the Month of Ailat, in the year 8718, Vulcan calendar, or the fiftieth day of Bocaj, in the year 3796, Andorian calendar.

Signed,

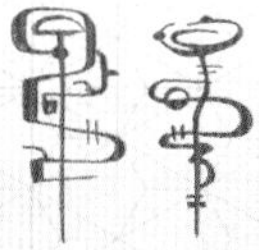

Soval
Ambassador
Representing the Vulcan People

Thy'lek Shran
Andorian High Guard
Representing the Andorian Empire

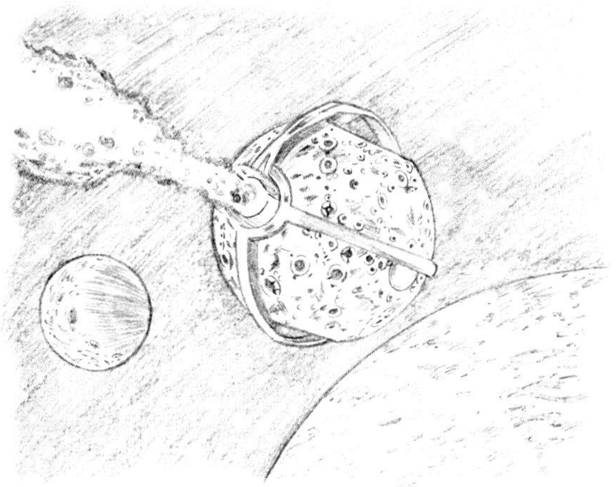

ABOVE: A rendering of the Xindi probe that attacked Earth.

The story of why that probe attacked Earth began centuries before—not just in another part of the Galaxy, but in another dimension entirely.

THE XINDI AND THE SPHERE BUILDERS

Not much is known about the race alternatively called "the Sphere Builders" and "the Guardians" other than they were technologically advanced and that they lived in another universe with a completely different molecular structure. "Conditions in their universe were becoming unlivable," wrote the Xindi historian J'Acov in *The Great Diaspora: The History of the Xindi*, "so they chose ours as their new home."

In order for the Sphere Builders to live in this universe, however, it was necessary to reconfigure it on a subatomic level. This reconfiguration would make it impossible for the life that currently existed in our universe to survive. To complete this project, the Sphere Builders constructed seventy-eight moon-sized spheres.

Through a technology that is still not fully understood, the spheres created a web of gravimetric energy that could put in motion the reconfiguration necessary to support their life-forms. This web became an area called the Delphic Expanse—2,000 light-years across and surrounded by thermobaric clouds that subspace communication could not penetrate. Thus many star systems and species in the Expanse were cut off from the rest of the Galaxy.

T'Pol, who was the only Starfleet scientist to examine the spheres, wrote in her log, "Left unhindered, the spheres eventually would not only reconfigure the Delphic Expanse, they would turn the entire universe into a space livable for the Sphere Builders, as well as making it unlivable for other life forms, including us."

OPPOSITE: A translated excerpt from the Xindi classic *Our Home*, a collection of stories written for Xindi children. The story excerpted here tells of the Arboreal child J'Acov's first encounter with an Avian on the final day of their planet. (J'Acov was also the name of the well-known Xindi historian who, as a child, survived the destruction of Xindus, but who would never confirm that this story was based on his own experiences.) **FOLLOWING SPREAD:** Jonathan Archer had several run-ins with Klingons, but the most serious was his intervention to help the Arin'Sen. They were a subject species of the Empire, and Archer succeeded in helping a ship of Arin'Sen refugees escape a Klingon ship's pursuit. Archer was eventually captured for this "crime," tried on the Klingon colony of Narendra III, and sentenced to life imprisonment on the penal asteroid Rura Penthe. He escaped, but the Klingons responded by putting a bounty on him, which technically was never lifted throughout his life.

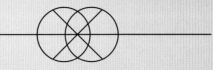

EXCERPT FROM XINDI DIASPORA CHILDREN'S BOOK

TRANSLATION

J'Acov and the Avian

. . . the ground shook, and J'Acov slipped. He gripped the doorway of the Avian home. Perched a thousand feet above the ground, he looked down; the footholds and outcroppings he'd used to climb up the impossibly thin stalk that supported the Avian dwelling seemed too small now to support him on the way back down. "Why did I climb up here?" he thought. "I'm an idiot!" He was frightened, and he could feel his tears coming.

He looked at the ground far below. From beneath the dirt, explosions; the Arboreal village was on fire. He didn't know what was happening. When the Reptilians had attacked before, the destruction had been caused by light from above, but now the explosions were coming from underground.

He heard a rumbling sound from above; he looked up to see a giant spaceship of the Aquatics. It hovered slowly overhead, a giant metal wing. Would they help him? Did they even see him? He was too terrified to call out, too afraid to let go of the doorway, and then the Aquatic ship was gone, off into the sky.

J'Acov looked down again, and saw another spaceship near the center of his village, and the Arboreals below trying to crowd inside. When his father told him they would be leaving on the spaceship, J'Acov hadn't accepted it. He couldn't imagine that they would actually ever leave their home. Now he saw the Tree of Family, home to so many Arboreals, consumed in flames. He should have listened.

He heard a flapping sound and looked up. An Avian! J'Acov had only seen them high up in the sky. He never realized how big their wings were. It flew directly at him, so fast that J'Acov was sure it would crash right into him. J'Acov had heard all the nightmare stories of Arboreal children being plucked from their homes by angry Avians, never to be seen again. He was sure he was about to die and closed his eyes in fear. The flapping sound stopped. J'Acov slowly opened his eyes.

The Avian halted inches from J'Acov. He saw the Avian's massive claws, which had locked onto one of the thick vines surrounding the dwelling. It stared angrily; J'Acov felt as if its bright eyes were cutting into his mind. Then the Avian spoke in a harsh rasp: "Why have thee invaded my home?"

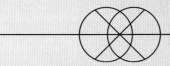

KLINGON BOUNTY ON ARCHER

TRANSLATED FROM THE KLINGON

WANTED!
JONATHAN ARCHER
HUMAN
MURDERER, TERRORIST

DESCRIPTION

Height: 1.84 meters

Weight: 81.7 kilograms

Remarks: Archer is commander of a rogue Human ship bent on the destruction of the Klingon Empire. He was last seen in the general vicinity of Xantoras. Approach with caution.

CAUTION

Jonathan Archer is an escaped felon. A renegade and terrorist, he is convicted of the most heinous crimes against the Klingon government. Archer is also a suspect in other terrorist attacks against other races throughout the galaxy.

REWARD

The Klingon High Council is offering a reward of up to 9,000 Darseks for information leading directly to the apprehension of Jonathan Archer. The full amount will be paid upon delivery of the felon, dead or alive.

Any member of the Klingon Military is authorized to function as an intermediary for the High Council and provide compensation for the execution of this bounty.

According to firsthand accounts from individuals who interacted with the Sphere Builders, among their technological advances was their ability to study future timelines. They saw that the biggest impediment to the completion of their plan was the future Federation. "And because they also foresaw that Earth would be a necessary component in the establishment of the Federation," J'acov wrote, "the Sphere Builders instituted a second plan to ensure the success of the first. They chose a world they could manipulate into becoming an enemy of Earth."

Their choice was Xindus, a planet within the Delphic Expanse. It was a unique world in that it developed six separate intelligent species: Arboreals, Aquatics, Insectoids, Reptilians, Primates, and Avians. The Sphere Builders manipulated the mythologies of all the species by visiting individual representatives of each species over the course of hundreds of years and presenting themselves as supernatural beings.

"The Guardian came to me," a Xindi Reptilian named Char'dus relayed in an oral tradition, "and told me our people, the Reptilians, were the true leaders of all the other species of the world." Similar myths among the other Xindi species asserted each species' natural hegemony. The only species that didn't believe the stories of the Sphere Builders/Guardians were the Xindi Avians, who refused to see wingless aliens as gods.

The Sphere Builders' influence on the other races, however, was profound, and a century-long war for domination of Xindus ensued that eventually resulted in the destruction of the planet. The Avian Xindi were obliterated into extinction. The other five species went out into space in what became known as the "Great Diaspora."

The Sphere Builders helped the Xindi navigate the Expanse and led them to a new home planet. The Sphere Builders then told the new Xindi Ruling Council (which comprised representatives of all the surviving species) that they had looked into the future and saw that beings from a planet called Earth would destroy the new Xindi home. It would be necessary to strike against Earth before the Humans could strike against the Xindi.

The once-warring Xindi species united under their new cause. A Xindi Primate named Degra designed a formidable weapon and tested the prototype against Earth itself in the belief that the Earthlings would not be able to trace the source of the probe.

They were wrong. Through a never-revealed source, Jonathan Archer found out not only that the Xindi—and ultimately the Sphere Builders—were responsible for the attack, but also their location in the Expanse. Despite the many tales of horror about previous ships that had entered the Expanse, *Enterprise* traveled there in a quest to find the Xindi and defeat the plans of the Sphere Builders. Archer and his crew were able to destroy the spheres, disrupting the gravimetric web. They eventually made allies of the Xindi, who many years later joined the Federation. As of this writing, the Sphere Builders were never heard from again.

IF YOU WANT PEACE, PREPARE FOR WAR

The attack on Earth would change Human affairs dramatically. Starfleet and the United Earth Government suddenly

LEFT: The only known image of a Xindi Avian.

realized how vulnerable they were. "We only had one ship to fight the battle with Xindi and [the Sphere Builders]," Admiral Forrest wrote in a memo to the United Earth Council. "If we don't make a commitment to build a Warp 5 fleet, we will be leaving ourselves open to other threats, and the next time we're attacked we might not prevail." The age of peace was over.

The experience with the Xindi also had a profound effect on Jonathan Archer personally. "When I left Earth," he said in a speech to Academy cadets many years later, "I was kind of a lighthearted explorer. The experience with the Xindi changed that. I lost that lightheartedness, but it was necessary. We have a role to fill, and we can't take it lightly."*

Archer wasn't the only one who had changed; the Xindi war put all Earthlings in a new frame of mind: if you want peace, be prepared for war. As it turned out, the timing of this change in Earth's attitude was fortuitous. The seed of the greatest conflict the Alpha Quadrant had ever faced was taking root.

THE ROMULANS

As is well known, the Vulcans were once an emotional, warlike people that found peace through their embrace of the teachings of Surak. But at some point after they discovered warp drive, a group of Vulcans who called themselves Romulans rejected the teachings of Surak and secretly left Vulcan to establish their own world. In the millennia of that intervening period, they developed a society that was warlike but by no means barbaric. The Romulans embraced the passions of emotion but also valued high culture and civility. They were ruled at first by an Imperial Senate, which appointed a praetor. By the 2100s, however, the praetor had usurped the power of the Senate and become a dictator.

For much of their history, the Romulans were primarily driven by a desire to protect themselves, and believed that the best way to do this was to expand their influence to neighboring star systems. To maintain control of these star systems, however, they needed more resources, so their expansion needed to continue. Thus, the Romulan Star Empire was born. Throughout this expansion, they managed to keep their origins and home planet's location secret to many of the advanced species in the Alpha Quadrant. No one outside the Empire knew what a Romulan looked like, including the Vulcans. But though the Vulcans had forgotten their distant brothers, the Romulans had not forgotten them.

---

*__AUTHOR'S NOTE:__ The experience in the Expanse also transformed Archer's impression of the role Earth would play in the future of the Galaxy. According to Archer, the difficulties with the Xindi were part of a larger conflict that he called "The Temporal Cold War" (TCW) that involved beings from the twenty-eighth, twenty-ninth, and thirty-first centuries, some of whom showed Archer future events through time travel. Archer did appear to have foreknowledge of the Earth's participation in forming the Federation, but he is our only source of information on the TCW. Many have doubted its plausibility, some even going so far as to say the assertions were symptoms of a messianic complex that compelled Archer to put himself at the center of history. "To employ a cliché," John Gill wrote, regarding the TCW's veracity, "only time will tell."

In 2153 the influential Minister V'Las became administrator of the Vulcan High Command. This appointment was, in fact, the fulfillment of a decades-long Romulan plot: V'Las was a Romulan who had replaced the real V'Las as a very young man. Over the decades that he had been a Vulcan minister, the Romulan was able to steer Vulcan on a course toward imperialism. "Controlling Earth and containing the Andorians were policies seemingly based in logic," wrote John Gill, "but looked at objectively, they were naked colonialism."

THE COALITION OF PLANETS

Enterprise's first years in space were considered an unqualified success. Because of the efforts of Jonathan Archer and his crew, Vulcan and Andoria had reached a peaceful settlement of their long conflict; the Tellarites, the pig-like species that valued arguing as a form of communication, also found themselves making peace with their enemies, the Andorians. United Earth Minister Nathan Samuels decided to capitalize on this success. In an attempt to form a strong, long-lasting alliance, he invited delegates from around the nearby galaxy to Earth to found the Coalition of Planets. Worlds that had kept to themselves—Rigel, Denobula, Coridan—were now sending delegates to Earth to become part of this grand adventure, but it almost ended before it began.

Terra Prime, the anti-alien group founded decades before on the fears of some Humans that aliens would invade and conquer their home, had lost its influence over the years as Earth saw the benefits of being part of the galactic community. That was until the Xindi attack. Anti-alien sentiment was again on the rise.

Terra Prime's leader, John Frederick Paxton, seized this opportunity. With new recruits, he landed on Mars and seized control of the verteron array, a powerful weapon Earth had developed to destroy stray asteroids and meteors. But the weapon could also destroy ships almost anywhere in the solar system. Paxton gave the aliens on Earth an ultimatum to leave immediately. "Fortunately," wrote Samuels in his autobiography, "there were too many people who would not let Earth slide back into a barbaric isolation." Paxton's plot was defeated.

A month after this final crisis was averted, the Coalition of Planets was incorporated. Though it was a step in the right direction, and a few of the Coalition members would also be founding members of the Federation, it would unfortunately take a much larger conflict to bring these worlds together permanently.

FOLLOWING SPREAD: The Romulan spy service, the Tal Shi'ar, replaced the real V'Las with their Romulan spy sometime in the mid-twenty-first century. As this counterfeit V'Las moved up the ranks of the High Command, he exercised an influence on Vulcan diplomacy while also providing his homeland with valuable intelligence. V'Las would send coded signals over subspace, which would then be decoded and transcribed on documents for the Romulan leaders. The following is the report regarding the first encounter between Romulans and Humans. The value of V'Las's position is apparent, as in this case he was able to include the Starfleet report on the incident, along with his own analysis.

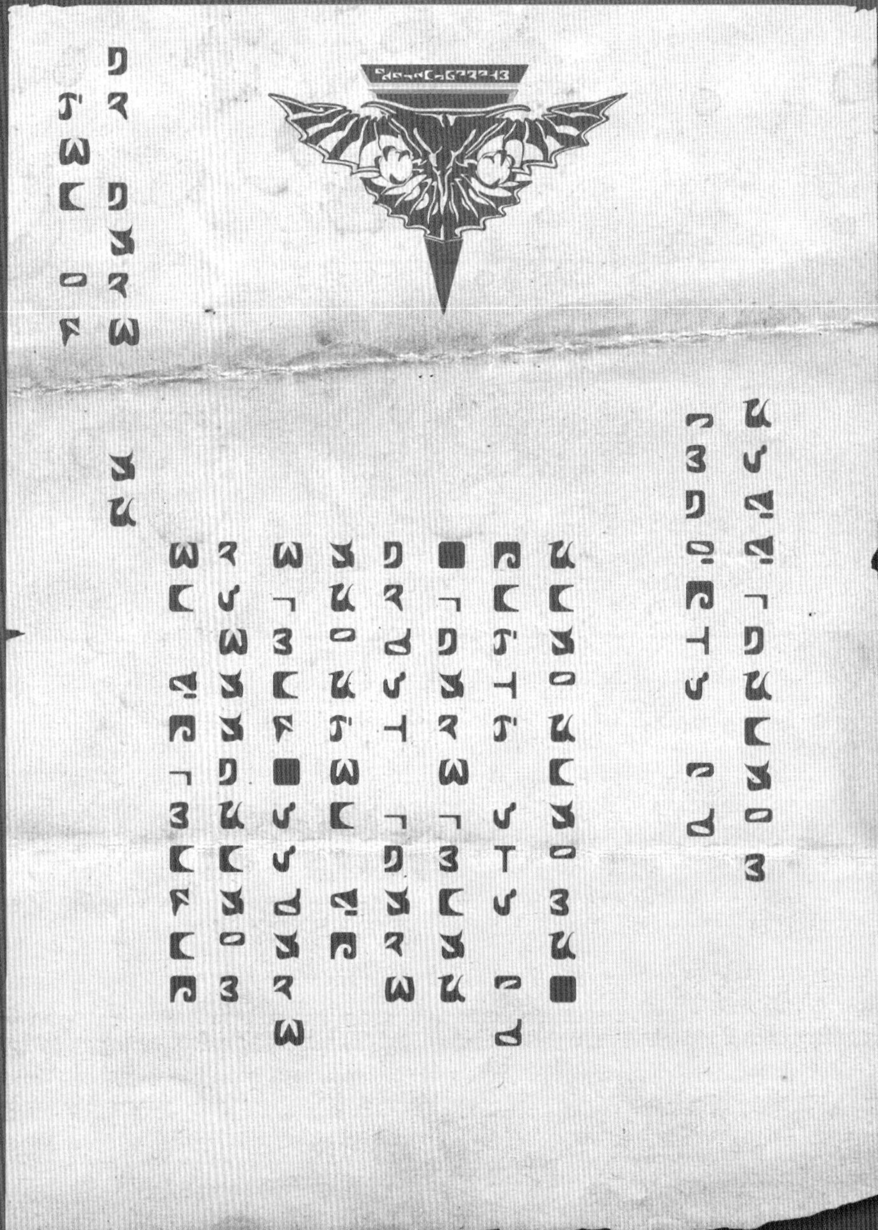

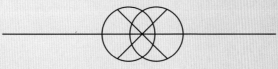

SECRET COMMUNIQUÉ FROM V'LAS TO ROMULAN TAL SHI'AR

TRANSLATED FROM THE ROMULAN

I have attached a copy of a report from the Earth Starfleet Command regarding the incident around Unroth III. As you will see, the Earth starship managed to gather a substantial amount of information regarding our mine technology. There are several things in this Starfleet report that should concern us.

1) The Earthmen were also able to penetrate our cloaking technology on the mines, though they were not able to do the same on our ships. But, as the report recommends, I have confirmed that Starfleet engineers have set to work on improving their quantum beacon technology to nullify our advantage in this area.

2) The Earthmen had the ability to understand our language. It is unclear how they did this, but it speaks to the unique abilities of at least one of their personnel and/or advanced computer processing capabilities to be able to so quickly and completely translate our spoken language.

3) The Earth starship was not destroyed, and they were able to quickly repair the damage to their ship. This shows a formidable resourcefulness and technical expertise if we should ever find ourselves in conflict with them.

Nowhere in the report does it mention any relationship between Vulcan and Romulus, and I have made further inquiries to confirm this. Fortunately, the Earth starship struck the minefield before they were able to descend to the planet, where they may have found our abandoned base, and the incident will at least temporarily guarantee that the Earthmen will not visit Unroth again.

CHAPTER II

THE ROMULAN WAR

2155–2160

"Before you declare to your people that a war is inevitable, ensure your own victory is as well."

—Gileus, praetor of the Romulan Empire, 2155

OPPOSITE: The Romulan destruction of Starbase 1 in 2156.

For a week during the negotiations of the charter for the Coalition of Planets, T'Jan, the Vulcan delegate, had held firm in her position. The Andorian Ambassador Thoris was becoming infuriated and Nathan Samuels was watching all his hard work come apart.

The delegates had met at the end of January 2155, and for most of February, negotiations to ratify the charter went smoothly. Samuels was able to bring the disparate species together to establish peace through trade, as well as agree on a workable structure to resolve disputes. He wanted, however, to go an extra step. He dubbed it the "my enemy is your enemy" clause: a clause that stated the worlds of the Coalition would join together to face common adversaries. All of the delegates were interested in this provision except T'Jan. As would be expected from a Vulcan, she was coldly logical and she unapologetically stated the position of her government. "We will not be held responsible," she said in a closed meeting of the delegates, "for the other members of this Coalition's irrational need to incite conflict."

"I thought Thoris was going to leap across the table," Samuels wrote in his unpublished memoirs. "As the arguments started to get out of control, I called a recess." Over the next week, Samuels had one-on-one meetings with the delegates to calm them down, but he could not prevail upon T'Jan to change her mind. So Samuels and the delegates returned to the table and Samuels withdrew the military alliance clause. "We accomplished so much," Samuels wrote. "I didn't want it to go out the window for something I expected I could get later."

The charter was ratified March 1, 2155. However, the fact that it was not a military alliance would have profound effects on the planet Earth.

THE ROMULAN PROBLEM

Although Samuels didn't know it then, the leader of the Romulan Empire, Praetor Gileus I, agreed that the Coalition of Planets could be on the cusp of a military alliance.*

Gileus was well aware of the Coalition negotiations, and they concerned him. Gileus had first been responsible for the attempt to bring Vulcan into the Empire, as well as the attempts to surreptitiously sow conflict between Andoria, Vulcan, and Tellar, all of which had backfired due to Human intervention. To him, Earth was Romulus's greatest threat.

BELOW: The portrait of Gileus I, which was used on Romulan currency. ***AUTHOR'S NOTE:** Recently, many internal Romulan documents have been smuggled out of the Empire. Among them are detailed government communiqués from this period, giving us a greater understanding of the actions of their leaders—and the motivations behind those actions—during the war.

"Senators," Gileus said in a speech to the Romulan Senate, "is it not clear that this so-called Coalition of Planets is nothing more than a euphemism for the Empire of Man?"

Although ambitious and cruel, Gileus was also a careful, intelligent ruler. Up until this time, he had made sure the Empire only challenged adversaries it was sure it could defeat: less advanced worlds with ample resources that could easily be controlled. To the life-forms on these worlds, Romulus was the most powerful force in the universe; they had no idea that there was anything as big or bigger than the Romulan Empire and thus never attempted to rebel. The Empire, however, was now at a crossroads. They continued to need new resources but bordered several potential adversaries who were now united. In a remarkably frank journal that Gileus secretly kept, he relates the problem he faced. (Gileus had written the journal as a day-to-day chronicle of the war for his son, who he expected would one day succeed him.)

"I know if I move against one, the others might easily fall in line to support it. But I understand power on Romulus relies on the comfort and prosperity of the people. If I deprive the people of these comforts, my political enemies will challenge my authority. I need to expand into someone else's territory in order to take control of their resources. I need a target that will both guarantee some of these resources and potentially undermine the Coalition."

In 2156, Earth presented him with one.

THE TRAGEDY OF STARBASE 1

For the three years previous to the signing of the Coalition Charter, Starfleet was already under way with one of their most ambitious plans: the Starbase Project. Recent circumstances had compelled Starfleet to recognize the need for bases outside the Sol system. The Utopia Planitia shipyard had a fleet of Warp 5 ships coming off the assembly line and a Warp 7 ship was already in the planning stages. It would be impractical for these ships to return to Earth when they needed servicing. In addition, the people of Earth had established colonies on remote worlds and expected Starfleet to protect these outposts. So work was under way to find habitable planets on which to build bases, as well as appropriate locations to build orbital facilities when a ground base was impractical.

Late in 2154, an uninhabited and unclaimed world forty-five light-years from Earth was chosen for the first of these bases, a planetoid around the red dwarf Algeron. However, the problem as to how to move the labor and material to build the base stood in the way of its completion until more Warp 5 ships were ready.

For this reason, Admiral Avram Gardner, the commander-in-chief of Starfleet, was impatient for more ships. In an internal memo to Nathan Samuels, he made the case for the vital need of starbases.

"There is no reason that we shouldn't share the base with our trading partners in the Coalition," wrote Gardner, "as long as Starfleet maintains the authority to run it as it sees fit. It seems to me that if we offer the base's facilities to any of our fellow Coalition members who agree to help transport resources and crews to Algeron, we may find there is some interest."

It was an understatement. Almost all of the species in the Coalition saw this as a potential asset for them. In

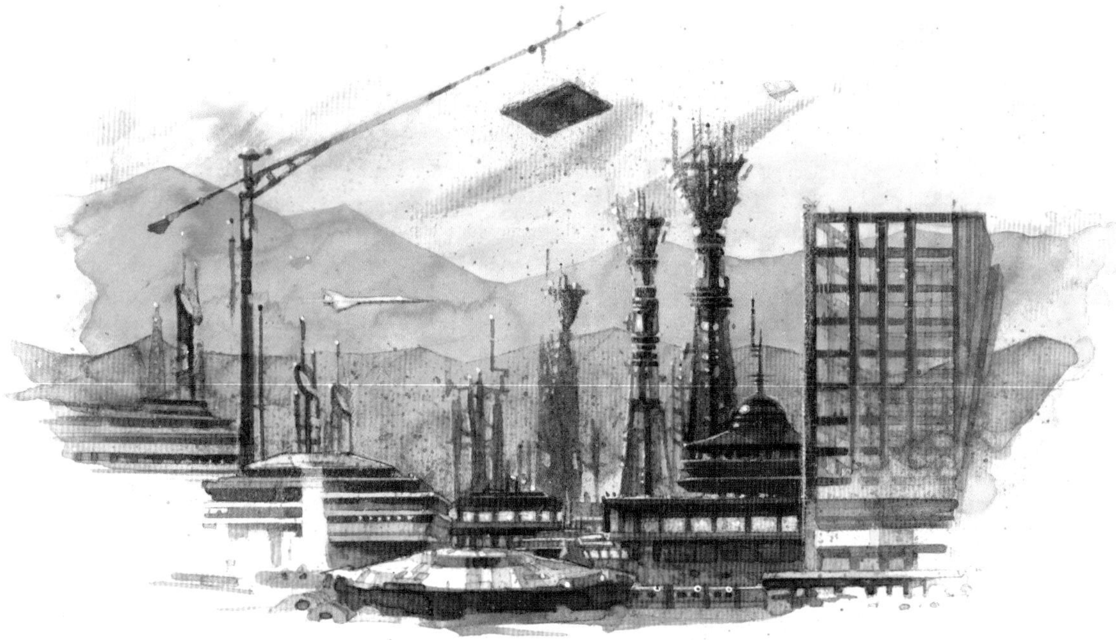

exchange for a usable base maintained by Earth, they only had to give up any claim to the planet it was built on. With the Coalition's cooperation, Gardner got quick approval from the United Earth Government to begin construction of Starbase 1.

Within a month Tellarite and Andorian ships, along with Earth's *Columbia* NX-02, had brought the first construction team to the planetoid. This group of technicians and engineers informally named themselves the "Starfleet Corps of Engineers." A year later, when they had finished the base and Gardner was looking to keep this efficient crew together to move them to a new project, the title was made official.

The base opened on February 8, 2156, and was a model for all the starbases that would come after it: clean, comfortable offices and homes around a state-of-the-art maintenance facility. Coalition planets began to use the base and it became a hub of activity and trade. By the time the base opened, work had already begun on Starbases 2 and 3. Despite the steady stream of alien traffic, the strict codes of conduct instituted by Starfleet made Starbase 1 an orderly, civilized outpost.

An outpost, it turned out, built on gold. An unusual magnetic field around the planet had kept superficial surveys by other species from detecting what was an enormously rich geologic deposit on this small planetoid, including castrodinium, a very dense substance used in construction of space habitats, and dilithium.

Starfleet engineers unearthed this treasure trove almost immediately upon breaking ground on the base. And since the Coalition allies had given up all claims to the planet,

ABOVE: Starbase 1, under construction in 2155.

that vein now belonged exclusively to Earth. It was the first time in history that Earth had its own source of these rare elements, and many species resented what they considered a wild stroke of luck for their Human colleagues. As it would turn out, the discovery was not lucky at all.

Algeron was located just outside the Romulan border, and because no one in this part of the Galaxy knew what Romulans looked like, Gileus was able to send Romulans disguised as Vulcans to the base to bring him an exhaustive amount of information about it. And the discovery of valuable resources on the planet set a plan in motion on Romulus. Gileus had his military prepare for war, and he brought in his naval chief of staff, Admiral Mindar, to personally plan an attack on this starbase and claim it for Romulus.

Mindar, however, was against this idea; a career officer, much older than Gileus, and the veteran of several wars of conquest, Mindar was hesitant to go to war with the Humans based on his impressions of what he'd heard and read of them. "In a limited number of years," Mindar wrote to a colleague after the war began, "the Humans have gone from being unknown in the Galaxy to being at its social and political center. That, in and of itself, made it a species we should have been more cautious about attacking." But Gileus wanted action, so his admiral followed orders.

On March 11, 2156, Gileus sent a subspace message in his name claiming that the Algeron system belonged to Romulus, and ordering Earth to vacate immediately. The intention was subtler than it seemed. The Romulans were a cause of concern to many species in the quadrant, and as a result of the message, several Coalition member governments ordered their ships to steer clear of Starbase 1. The United Earth Government, on the other hand, had made a large investment of time and resources establishing the base, so Starfleet held its ground. All this played right into Gileus's hand.

"I knew the details of the [Coalition] charter," Gileus wrote in his journal to his son. "I knew the other members were not required to join a war on Earth's behalf." By claiming the system, he accurately predicted that Earth would not readily abandon its base, and that non-Earth ships would soon stay away.

After the threat from Gileus, Gardner lobbied hard for a stronger military presence in the Algeron system, but Samuels and the ministers of Earth, with the memory of the destruction caused by the Xindi war fresh in their minds, resisted initiating an action that might unintentionally start a war. Gardner, frustrated by the inaction and worried about his personnel on a vulnerable base, sent the *Columbia* NX-02 and the new *Excalibur* NX-03 to the area for "scheduled maintenance."

The next step for the Romulans was a surprise attack on Starbase 1. Planned to occur two months after the warning, it gave aliens enough time to give Starbase 1 a wide berth, so the attack would affect Earth forces alone. Taking over the planet would serve two purposes: Romulus would gain badly needed resources and it would have an accurate test of the willingness of the Humans to fight.

On May 18, 2156, a fleet of five Romulan warbirds under the command of Admiral Mindar entered the Algeron system. The NX-02, under the command of Fleet Captain Erika Hernandez, and the *Excalibur*, under the command of Captain Bran Stiles, immediately saw that they were

hopelessly outmatched. The Romulans were jamming all communications with Earth, so Hernandez ordered Stiles to escape the system and warn Starfleet Command. Stiles was reluctant to leave *Columbia* alone to defend the base, but followed his orders and left the system. Two of the Romulan ships broke off from the attack to pursue *Excalibur*, while *Columbia* fought the remaining three. Outgunned and outmatched, *Columbia* was quickly lost with all hands. The three Romulan ships moved in and destroyed the base, then landed ground troops to fortify their position and root out any survivors. By the end of the day, the Romulan flag was planted in the center in what had been called Main Street on the base.

Meanwhile, *Excalibur* could not escape the jamming of the two Romulan ships in pursuit. The lone survivor of *Excalibur*, first officer Bryce Shumar, relayed what happened in an oral history of the war published on its fifth anniversary. "Captain Stiles knew that the Romulans were faster at warp, and that eventually we would be run down and have to engage in ship-to-ship battle. He also knew our chances were slim against two Romulan ships, and it was paramount that Earth be warned."

LEFT: "The Victory of Algeron," a painting commissioned for the senate chambers. At war's end it was quietly taken down. **OPPOSITE:** The following excerpts from the *Columbia*'s ship's transcription record, or "black box," were discovered many years after the Romulan conflict. The record survived the destruction of the *Columbia* and was found in a wide orbit around Algeron.

Personal Log, May 12, 2156, Assistant Engineer Rick Stiles recording. We've just arrived at the Algeron system for maintenance. The Excalibur, under the command of Bran Stiles, is also in orbit here. I haven't seen Uncle Bran . . . I mean, Captain Stiles . . . since before he took command of Excalibur. Maybe if we get shore leave I'll run into him on the Starbase.

Captain's Log, May 18, 2156, Erika Hernandez recording. Long-range sensors have detected five Romulan ships, on a direct course for Algeron. It now seems clear that my friend Jonathan Archer was right, that the Romulan statement declaring this system part of their empire was a prelude to an attack. They will arrive in forty-five minutes, and are already jamming our subspace frequencies. I've sent a message by shuttlepod to the Excalibur ordering it to leave orbit and warn Starfleet Command. I'm somewhat relieved that the Romulans are jamming our frequencies; I don't want to have an argument with Captain Stiles, who I am sure will want to stay and fight. But there would be no point.

Personal Log . . . guess it's still the 18th . . . Rick Stiles, this is Rick Stiles . . . I'm in the catwalk . . . the catwalk next to the port nacelle . . . Romulans hit us pretty hard . . . Chief Engineer Rivers sent me up here with a repair team . . . They're dead . . . my team's dead . . . it's on fire . . . bulkhead is sealed, must be vacuum below . . . comm system, tried the comm system, no one answers . . . found this tricorder . . . I don't know what to do . . . saw Uncle Bran yesterday . . . he called me, called the captain and asked to talk to me . . . it was good to see him . . . didn't get to see the base . . .

MEMORY ALPHA LCARS HARD COPY EXTRACT

ORIGINAL SOURCE: UNITED SOL SYSTEM INFORMATION NETWORK	18.5.2156

STARBASE 1 ATTACKED!

Romulans destroy two Starfleet ships, occupy base

By Gannet Brooks

May 18, 2156—In a stunning, devastating attack, the Romulan Empire moved against Starbase 1, on a planetoid in the Algeron system, killing more than 700 people and destroying the base and two Starfleet ships, the *Columbia* NX-02 and the *Excalibur* NX-03. The attack came without warning.

"This is a sad day," Nathan Samuels, administrative minister of the United Earth Council, told reporters, "the result, I am sure, of a tragic misunderstanding. We of the United Earth Council are doing everything we can to make sure this does not escalate into a full-scale war." Samuels said that the United Earth Government had given the Romulans an opening to explain this attack. If the explanation was not satisfactory, then United Earth would be forced to take action. As of this writing, there has been no response from the Romulans.

The news of the attack was delayed reaching Earth. At 7:48am Pacific Standard Time, Starfleet Headquarters received a communication from an *Excalibur* shuttlepod in the Gamma Hydra system. The shuttlepod had a lone occupant, Lt. Commander Bryce Shumar, first officer of the *Excalibur*. He relayed news of the attack, which had occurred several hours earlier. Lt. Shumar is the only known survivor of the attack. The ships had crew complements of fifty-seven each; the base was manned by 450 members of Starfleet, many of whom had families that lived with them on the base, bringing the total base population to 600.

In recent weeks, Starbase 1 had become the subject of a dispute between Earth and Romulus, with the Romulan praetor, Gileus, claiming the planet as part of his Empire.

As the *Excalibur* approached the border of the Gamma Hydra system, Stiles ordered his science officer to scan ahead for any comet magnitude five or greater. "The captain gambled that the Romulan sensors wouldn't be able to penetrate the tail of a comet," Shumar said. They discovered one, and Stiles ordered his helm to alter course for it. "He then ordered me to take a subspace buoy into a shuttlepod." Stiles brought *Excalibur* out of warp directly into the comet's tail. The Romulan sensors momentarily lost *Excalibur*. "Once we were in the tail of the comet, *Excalibur* launched my shuttlepod," Shumar said, "and *Excalibur* left, heading off in a different direction.

"The captain guessed that the Romulans would assume he'd used the comet in an attempt to lose them." As *Excalibur* successfully led the Romulans away, Shumar flew the shuttlepod out of the comet's tail, launched the subspace relay buoy, and contacted Starfleet.

"I was in that shuttlepod for two days," Shumar said, "wondering what happened to *Excalibur*." It was *Enterprise* that rescued him. "I hadn't met [Jonathan] Archer before, but the question was barely out of my mouth when I could read the answer in his face." *Excalibur* had been destroyed. As it turned out, Stiles's effort to warn Starfleet as soon as possible made no difference to the outcome of the battle, but choosing Shumar to survive would affect the outcome of the war.

SAMUELS'S MISTAKE

When the news of the attack on Starbase 1 reached Earth, there were two very different reactions. At Starfleet, Admiral Gardner immediately wanted Earth to declare war on Romulus. But the United Earth Council saw things differently. "We have to take responsibility for the fact that two of our ships in orbit of the planet provoked them," Minister Samuels said in a meeting of the Council. A slim majority of the Council agreed, and asked for Gardner's resignation as commander of starfleet. Admiral Rafael Douglas was promoted in his place. Douglas, an orderly and detail-driven man, gave the impression that he would be more cautious in his dealings with the Romulans.

With the belief that the attack was a misunderstanding or reaction to provocation, Nathan Samuels immediately set out to diplomatically engage the Romulans. He sent a subspace message on the same channel that Gileus had used, sternly objecting to the Romulan attack with this warning: "I seek immediate discussion with the leaders of Romulus, or Earth will be forced to take difficult action."

The statement was meant to be a threat; instead, the Romulans perceived it as an invitation. "I did not expect so weak a response from the Earthmen," Gileus wrote. "They were clearly irresolute and could be wiped out much more easily than I had initially believed." He immediately sent his ships back with the intention of destroying the rest of the Human fleet and isolating the Human homeworld in preparation of an attack. "There's no doubt," Gileus wrote in his journal, "we will win."

OPPOSITE: Though newspapers were long out of use, this article, published digitally over the worldwide computer service, was read by over two billion people within the first ten minutes of it being posted.

EARTH AND ROMULUS GO TO WAR

Romulan ships quickly made bold attacks against Earth's ships. *Enterprise* found itself engaged in a battle at Galorndan Core against two Romulan battle cruisers. But *Enterprise* was Starfleet's most battle-hardened ship and crew, and managed to destroy one of the ships and damage the other before successfully getting away.

Romulan ships also attacked ships carrying dilithium, castrodinium, and trititanium to Earth. Class-J starships, still in service, provided easy targets for the Romulan battle cruisers. The Romulans were very careful to only attack cargo vessels on their way *to* Earth, so as to never threaten the property on its way to other Coalition planets.

Losses were heavy. On June 1, 2156, Samuels, finally understanding the reality of his situation, declared that Earth was at a state of war with the Romulan Empire. The United Earth Council tasked Admiral Douglas and Starfleet with winning it.

Despite the Council's previous policies, Douglas hadn't been sitting idly by; he had long expected this, and had been making preparations. Since the attack on Starbase 1, Starfleet had been inundated with requests from people wanting to enlist. Douglas had been quietly aggressive about cherry-picking individuals with valuable skills, especially engineers, whom he immediately sent to Utopia Planitia to help finish the other Warp 5 ships under construction. This influx of labor was directly responsible for two more Warp 5 ships coming off the assembly line less than three weeks after war was declared. Douglas knew he needed them.

In an internal Starfleet memo to the rest of the Admiralty, Douglas laid out three clear problems Earth faced in prosecuting the war: "1) We don't know where the Romulan homeworld is, which prevents us from retaliating at the heart of their Empire. 2) We have no allies in the war. 3) We don't know what Romulans look like, which makes it difficult or nearly impossible to curtail Romulan spying."

For the first problem, Douglas knew the Romulans had a huge advantage: no one knew where their home was. The borders of the Empire were well defined, but Douglas presumed (correctly) that those borders were far away from the center of power. Though he couldn't waste ships and labor on a vain search for this secret world, Douglas knew he needed to put as many ships as possible outside of the Sol system to take advantage of any intelligence that came his way regarding the location of Romulus.

The three Warp 5 ships, *Enterprise*, *Constellation*, and *Atlantis*, were not ordered to return to Earth to defend the Sol system as other ships were. The two new Warp 5 vessels, *Defiant* and *Lexington*, would also stay outside of the Sol system. Earth would have to be defended by the slower ships in the fleet. Douglas also put Admiral Gardner in command of Starbase 2, an orbital facility near the Betreka nebula, so that a commander with experience would be in the forward area.

Regarding the second problem, Douglas knew there was little likelihood that any Coalition planets would openly join the military effort. But because the Romulans had been attacking shipping and the Warp 5 ships were being kept out on the frontier, Douglas had no effective way to supply these ships on the front lines. The only feasible solution in that regard was the Coalition. For this, Douglas went to Samuels. "I knew this couldn't be an official request,"

Samuels wrote in his memoirs, "but I also knew that the other Coalition members recognized the hard fact that Earth was taking on an Empire that threatened all of them. If we won, they all won."

Most of the Coalition members saw the logic of this argument. Vulcans, Andorians, and Tellarites immediately agreed to ship food and medical supplies to Starfleet vessels fighting the war, and, later, to secretly supply ordnance and spare parts.

Regarding the final problem—the Romulans' spy network and the mystery of their appearance—Douglas laid out his plan in the same memo: "It is clear from the attack on Earth and Starbase 1, as well as their knowledge of the cargo shipping routes, that the Romulans have a very competent spy network."

Douglas proposed strict security guidelines for Earth and any bases and colonies. Samuels got the United Earth Council to go along. The measures, laid out in a United Earth Government directive, were draconian: "1) Every alien on Earth or one of its colonies is to be registered and confirmed as a member of the species it represents through medical testing. 2) Any alien whose identity the authorities cannot verify is to be detained. 3) Said alien's government will be directed to remove that alien from Earth or its bases or colony."

It was ironic that, only a few years before, Samuels had helped fight off the bigoted elements who sought to eject aliens from Earth. He now presided over the largest government-sponsored wave of anti-alien paranoia in the planet's history. A propaganda campaign was begun, elevating the public's fear of these intergalactic "monsters."

On the face of it, it looked as if Starfleet didn't stand a chance in a one-on-one battle with the Romulans. The Romulans had had warp drive for much longer, so it was assumed that they had a much larger, more advanced fleet than Earth. But maintaining an Empire had its costs, and the Romulans needed to properly allocate their resources. Before the war with Earth, their military leaders did not think the Romulans needed fast ships to keep order on the primitive planets that were under their control. Most of their considerable fleet was made up of large, slow ships used to move passengers and material, only armed with weaponry useful for attacking either planetary targets or slow-moving primitive spacecraft.

Still, at the beginning of the war Romulus had fifteen Warp 5 battle cruisers to Earth's five, and that advantage should have been enough to guarantee a Romulan victory. If Gileus had obeyed a strategy of attrition, he would have eventually won. But he wanted to strike at Earth with one large, decisive blow. This strategy was his undoing.

THE OCCUPATION OF DENOBULA

One of the first species to visit Earth after the Vulcans were the Denobulans. This unique species was technologically advanced and could be either peaceful or warlike. Confined to the one continent on their home planet, with living space at a premium, Denobulans valued strong and complicated familial bonds. But to the Romulans, the Denobulans mattered for only one reason: At warp speed the Denobulan system was only a few days away from Sol.

"Mindar tells me that for Romulan ships to attack the Human homeworld," Gileus wrote, "they need a staging area."

REMEMBER,
ENTERPRISE
YOU MAY BE TALKING TO A ROMULAN!

Heavy cruisers traveling the distance from Romulus to Earth at high warp for weeks would be at a huge disadvantage if they also needed to engage in battle. Gileus decided to use the Denobulan system as his staging area. "One might think that we will give up the advantage by giving the Earthmen warning," Gileus wrote, "but I have complete knowledge of Earth's defense systems. Surprise is not necessary."

Because the Denobulans were not at war with Romulus—nor allied with Earth—Gileus and his military advisers projected that they would be unprepared for an attack and easily subdued. The Romulan ships could move in, rest, be serviced, and then travel the two days to Earth and completely wipe it out. He placed the mission under the command of his greatest warrior, Admiral Mindar.

But if Mindar was reticent about the initial attack on Starbase 1, he was even less enthusiastic about a campaign to the Sol system. "With all due respect, we had months to prepare for the attack on the Earth base," Mindar wrote to his praetor in a memo. "To give me only two weeks to come up with a battle plan for the invasion of Target One [Earth] seems ill advised." Though many spies had corroborated all the information Mindar used on Starbase 1, he only had the one source—Minister V'Las of Vulcan—for the information about Earth. But, again, he followed his orders.

On October 1, 2158, after traveling for three weeks at Warp 5, ten Romulan battle cruisers entered the Denobulan system. The Denobulans had an orbiting spaceport, which the Romulans immediately boarded. They proceeded to kill every Denobulan on it. Mindar knew he had a planet full of Denobulans to be dealt with and that they had a reputation for being fierce fighters when they needed to be. He would need to give them pause in any consideration of interfering with the Romulans while they used the Denobulan facilities to prepare their vessels. He sent a short subspace message to the Denobulan center of power: "Do not interfere, or this attack will only be the first." He then ordered his ships to fire on the Denobulan continent. The attack was devastating; over three million Denobulans were killed. It served its purpose. The Denobulans would be occupied with this catastrophe for far longer than Mindar needed to get his ships ready.

By this time, Admiral Douglas at Starfleet was well aware that there was a Romulan attack force two days away from Earth, and he hoped that the preparations he had made were enough.

THE BATTLE OF SOL

Mindar was correct to be concerned about his intelligence on Earth. Gileus had trusted that V'Las had provided up-to-date intelligence on the Sol System's defensive precautions. However, since the Vulcan stewardship of Earth had ended and the two planets were now in an equal partner alliance, the Vulcan government was less aggressive in gaining knowledge of Earth's security precautions. And United Earth—especially Starfleet under command of Admiral Douglas—was not sharing any more information than necessary.

The Romulan fleet had three targets. The first was the verteron array on Mars. Generally considered to be the

OPPOSITE: A popular propaganda poster from the war that appeared all over Earth, translated into many languages.

center of Earth's defenses, the array's original purpose was to use the power of the faster-than-light particles to divert comets and asteroids in the solar system. However, verterons, when accelerated, could also be very destructive. The Romulans knew the array could target a ship or planet almost anywhere in the solar system. Their first move was to come out of warp very near Mars and quickly destroy the array.

The second target, which was to be hit simultaneously, was the shipyard of Utopia Planitia, also on Mars. Earth had stepped up starship production as part of the war effort, and there were now six more Warp 5 ships in various stages of construction. If these ships were completed, Earth would be closer to equal with Romulus. If they were destroyed, the loss would be insurmountable.

The third target was Earth. "I believe once we destroy Earth, morale will be crushed," Gileus wrote, "and the remaining Humans in the Galaxy will lose the will to fight." Knowing the other Warp 5 ships had not been recalled to Earth, Gileus believed that once the verteron array was destroyed, his fleet of ten of Romulus's most advanced ships could easily take on whatever vessels Starfleet still had in the system. The war would soon be over.

The ten Romulan ships came out of warp just above Mars, and, as planned, the fleet immediately split. Within minutes, five of the ships had successfully destroyed the verteron array, while the other five, headed by Mindar, moved into a geosynchronous orbit over Utopia Planitia.

After the battle of Sol and before his execution, Mindar demanded the Romulan Right of Statement, an ancient tradition wherein a convicted criminal is allowed to record the reasons for his crime in as much detail as he wants. This statement was part of an immense package of material later smuggled out of Romulus. "I was concerned," Mindar said in his statement, "when our scans of the shipyard showed only a few superstructures. My initial thought was that our intelligence had overestimated Starfleet ship production." At the moment, however, he had to proceed with his orders. His fleet destroyed the shipyard.

This was the first piece of the Romulans' plan that went wrong, and using Denobula as a staging area was the cause. When Starfleet Command detected the Romulan ships heading toward Denobula, Douglas guessed that it was a prelude to an invasion of Sol. His first order was the evacuation of all ships and personnel from Utopia Planitia. Any ship that could lift off on its own was ordered to, and other ships in the solar system were ordered to Mars to tow those that couldn't move under their own power. Even half-finished constructs lifted off or were towed via grapplers from other ships. This ragtag fleet left the Mars orbit for a hiding place behind the Ceres asteroid. The Romulans were far too distant from Earth to detect the migration. Thus, the shipyard that Mindar destroyed was completely empty.

After destroying the verteron array and the Utopia Planitia shipyard, the Romulans broke orbit and set a course for Earth. But as soon as they did, one of Mindar's ships was hit with a powerful verteron beam, completely destroying it. "I was stunned," Mindar said in his statement. "I had seen the verteron array on Mars destroyed with my own eyes." He had no idea where the beam could be coming from.

What he and Gileus did not—could not—know was that the verteron array on Mars was no longer the center of Earth's defenses. Years earlier, after the Mars array had been hijacked by the Terra Prime movement, Starfleet decided it was too vulnerable. So without the knowledge of even their closest allies they constructed a second verteron array on the surface of Venus. Hidden under Venus's dense cloud cover, and operated remotely from Earth, it was the best-kept secret of Earth's defenses. It was that verteron array that was now firing on Mindar's fleet.

Under attack, Mindar's ships immediately broke formation. Two more were destroyed before the remainder of the fleet moved to a blind spot directly behind Mars, which Mindar's science officer calculated the beam couldn't reach.

But while Mindar considered his limited options, a fleet of a dozen Earth ships came out of warp. The *S.S. Intrepid*, commanded by the newly promoted Captain Bryce Shumar, having just helped to take the Utopia Planitia ships to their hiding place, now led other ships in an attack on the Romulans. "Our ships were much slower than the Romulans'," Shumar said in the same oral history in which he described surviving the *Excalibur*'s destruction. "But we neutralized that advantage. They were penned in. Any attempt to move out from behind Mars made them a target of the verteron array on Venus." Shumar then pressed the attack very aggressively, taking personal satisfaction in the battle. "Douglas had told me to keep our distance, keep risks at a minimum, but I . . . well, I pushed our fleet pretty hard, and when I watched that first Romulan ship blow up . . . look, I wanted payback, and I got it."

Watching his fleet decimated, Mindar ordered a retreat. As the Romulans tried to move out of the system and go to warp, the Starfleet ships managed to inflict more damage; several of Mindar's ships were too compromised to retreat. "Rather than be captured," Mindar stated, "I ordered them to self-destruct according to Romulan tradition."

Mindar came to the Sol system with ten warbirds, but left with four. It was a crushing defeat from which the Romulans would never completely recover. Six of their fastest, most advanced starships had been destroyed in one battle. Starfleet didn't know it at the time, but this put Earth on an almost equal footing with the Romulans. And the memory of the battle would live on well past the end of the war. Although Human beings would make plenty of enemies in the coming years, the outcome of the Battle of Sol has, for the last 150 years, prevented any alien species from attempting to attack Earth.

On Romulus, the news of the failed attack on Sol was greeted with rage by its praetor. Gileus now had a total of only nine heavy cruisers. When Mindar returned, Gileus ordered his execution. It was one of many mistakes Gileus made that ultimately led to his downfall. Mindar, despite his defeat, had been a valuable asset.

Although Gileus had many ships in his fleet, most of them were not fast enough to be effective in the war against Earth. And having seen that even his most advanced heavy cruisers were not enough to defeat Earth, Gileus decided to not only order the building of more ships, but also require that those ships have a technological advantage that the Earthlings could not readily overcome.

CHERON

Well before the war, when Romulans encountered an Earth ship for the first time, they had a unique advantage: they could cloak their ships so as to be invisible. But Starfleet had encountered cloaking technology previously, and by the time the war began it had neutralized this advantage to such an extent that the Romulans did not attempt to use it. But now Gileus wanted to try to utilize the technology again, and he returned to the planet that had initially provided him with this tool.

In the southernmost part of the galaxy was the planet Cheron. Though it was within the borders of the Romulan Empire, the planet was too advanced to be easily conquered, so it had the unique status of Romulan ally. Though technologically advanced, Cheron was socially primitive; one-half of its population was subservient to the other based on the color of their skin. As a result, the planet's ruling elite did not want their hegemony compromised. In exchange for Romulus's protection, resources, and guarantee of non-interference, they provided their expertise in shipbuilding, which was based on their utilization of slave labor. After the defeat at Sol, Gileus turned to them, promising Cheron a large reward if the shipbuilders could improve the cloaking technology so that it would be impervious to the Starfleet sensors.

If he had even one ship that could move undetected in enemy territory, Gileus believed he could once again turn the tide of war. He diverted all potential resources to the project. In one of the last entries in the journal to his son, he confided his thinking on this decision. "I know it will place a greater burden on the remaining ships of the fleet and it will create shortages on the homeworld. This is the political risk. But it will be worth it, as in three months' time, my invisible ship will destroy the homeworld of the Humans while Romulus's location stays a secret, making a counterattack impossible." Unfortunately for Gileus, he was wrong on both counts.

VULCAN'S SECRET

Fifty years before the Romulan War with Earth, a Vulcan archaeologist named T'Pek, examining the ruins of an ancient site, found evidence of a rebellious group of Vulcans that had wanted to embrace their emotions and reject the teachings of Surak. They had left Vulcan over a millennium before, to start anew on another world. This group charted their intended destination before they left, and the archaeologist discovered an ancient tome, called *Vulcana's Betrayal,* detailing their plan. The planet's location was included in the tome, along with the name the group had chosen for

OPPOSITE: Many lives were lost and families destroyed by the Romulan conflict. Starfleet had a policy carried over from the armed forces of a nation-state on Earth: that no one family should carry an undue burden of the war. When casualty reports came to Earth in the first weeks of the war, several members of the Stiles family were among them. Bran Stiles had been captain of the *Excalibur* and his nephew Rick Stiles an engineer aboard *Columbia*; both were killed at the attack on Starbase 1. Bran's daughter, Commander Phyllis Stiles, was a casualty on the freighter *Fortunate Son* when it was destroyed in a Romulan attack, and her brother, Andre Stiles, science specialist aboard the *Enterprise,* was also killed. When this was brought to Admiral Douglas's attention, he saw that there was one Stiles family member still serving in Starfleet, Terry Stiles, Bran's brother and father to Rick. He immediately ordered him home. Douglas's order came a day too late.

Captain's log, *S.S. Intrepid*
October 10, 2156

Bryce Shumar recording. We have successfully fought off the Romulan fleet. Six of the ten Romulan warbirds were destroyed. The surviving four went to warp one hour ago, and I've only now surmised that they're not coming back. The ship will remain at Red Alert until we're certain. The Intrepid suffered major damage which our engineers are repairing as we head back to Earth on impulse power. I regret to inform Starfleet Command that I am unable to carry out the order I received minutes before the attack began; one of our casualties was Terry Stiles, the ship's chef, whom Admiral Douglas had ordered home. Terry was a good crewman who was lending a hand in the torpedo room when it suffered a direct hit from a Romulan salvo.

their new world: *Rom A'losh*, meaning in ancient Vulcan, "Raptor's Nest."

Buried in the archaeologist's long treatise, this piece of academic information wasn't considered particularly interesting when it was initially discovered. It had been duly presented to the Vulcan Science Academy and catalogued in its library. However, when war broke out between Earth and Romulus, a member of the Academy, a scientist named Skon (son of the first Vulcan ambassador to Earth), recalled reading this treatise and pulled it out. "Logic suggests to me that this is in fact the origin of the Romulans," he relayed in a letter written to a fellow Vulcan, "and that they are our distant brothers."

The person to whom Skon wrote was a close family acquaintance, T'Pau. A former leader of the Syrannites, a group that helped bring the original teachings of Surak back to the center of governing principles, she was now a member of the Vulcan High Council. T'Pau logically concluded that if the Romulans were related to Vulcans there could easily be Romulan spies in the government.

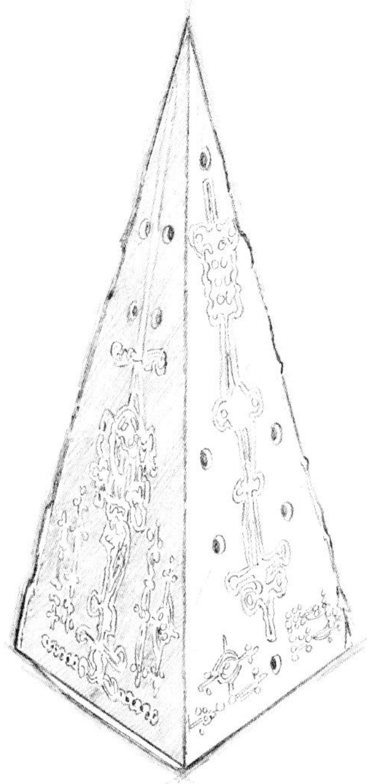

She was correct: V'Las, though no longer administrator of the Vulcan High Command (which had been dissolved), still had influence with many members of the Vulcan High Council.

So, instead of bringing the information to the High Council, she found a covert way to get it to Earth.

She contacted Commander T'Pol, the Vulcan science officer still serving on *Enterprise*. (Though Vulcan was not at war with Romulus, the High Council had granted T'Pol's request to continue to serve as first officer on a Starfleet vessel.) *Enterprise* then secretly relayed the information back to Earth.

Admiral Douglas now had extremely vital information for the war effort. With the location of the Romulan homeworld, he could finally take the war to Romulus.

But he had to be careful; Douglas knew he also had information that that could be extremely incendiary. Human propaganda had done a very good job of painting the Romulans as monsters. If it were discovered that they were essentially Vulcans, Humans would have difficulty trusting their longtime allies. The information could have permanently destroyed the Vulcan/Human alliance. So, thanks to Douglas, the source of how he obtained the location of Romulus was quietly buried. Only a few people on Earth and Vulcan would know the truth; the rest of the Federation would have no idea of the Vulcan/Romulan relationship for more than one hundred years.

Even with the new and valuable information regarding the location of Romulus, Douglas would need to proceed

ABOVE: The Kir'shara, the original writings of Surak, whose rediscovery put Vulcan back on a path toward logic and peace.

carefully. His intelligence network had told him of the importance of the shipyards at Cheron. But he hadn't attacked them because of Cheron's distance; to detail enough ships to cripple the shipyards would give the Romulans enough time to send a force to defend it. He would need another target, equally important, to split their forces. Now that he knew the location of Romulus, he had it.

THE BATTLE OF CHERON

Douglas ordered Gardner to take command of the forward task force, comprising three out of four of Earth's remaining Warp 5 ships: *Atlantis*, *Enterprise*, and *Defiant*. (The only ship not included was *Lexington*. *Constellation* had been damaged successfully defending Starbase 2, and was being repaired.) On January 10, 2160, these ships immediately set course for Cheron, with the mission to destroy the shipyards. The Romulans easily surmised their plan and sent forces to intercept them. Douglas had expected this, and his experience with the Romulans taught him that they sought to have a vastly superior force. If Starfleet committed three of its advanced ships to a battle, the Romulans would commit the bulk of their war fleet. He was proven right immediately; Gileus sent seven of his nine heavy cruisers to protect the shipyards. Not unexpectedly, Starfleet was outgunned, but Douglas gambled that the second part of his plan would save his fleet from destruction.

The Earth ships reached Cheron and were almost immediately engaged by the Romulan ships, which arrived much sooner than expected. When they did, Gardner, on board *Defiant*, sent a signal to *Lexington*, which was stationed several light-years away, just outside the Romulan border. As the Starfleet ships engaged the Romulans at Cheron, *Lexington* was joined by several Denobulan warships. Because of the attack on their homeworld, Denobula had been convinced by Samuels to join the war effort with Earth. The small fleet set course for Romulus.

The battle raged at Cheron. It was three Starfleet ships against seven Romulan ships. "We knew this was going to be the decisive battle," Jonathan Archer said in an oral history of the war. "We knew that we might not return from it, so we fought all that much harder." They destroyed two of the Romulan ships before they lost *Defiant*, and Admiral Gardner with it.

The other two Starfleet ships would have almost certainly been destroyed had it not been for a panicked call to the Romulan fleet from its praetor. "Return to Romulus! Protect your home!" It was Gileus's own voice coming through the comm channels of the Romulan ships. Upon receiving this direct order from his praetor, the leader of the Romulan task force, a less experienced admiral named Tal, reluctantly took three of his ships and headed for Romulus. Now the tide of

---

FOLLOWING SPREAD: The following transcription from the ancient Vulcan text *Vulcana's Betrayal* was discovered by the archaeologist T'Pek. "Vulcana" is a reference not to the planet, but to the mother god of Vulcan mythology. "The Dissembler" refers to Surak, whom these ancient Vulcans considered a kind of religious con man who had sought the destruction of their way of life. "Seer" is an ancient Vulcan word that referred to an astronomer, and "Death's Eye" refers to Shariel, the Vulcan God of Death. Shariel was a constellation in the Vulcan sky, and his "eye" was the topmost star in the constellation.

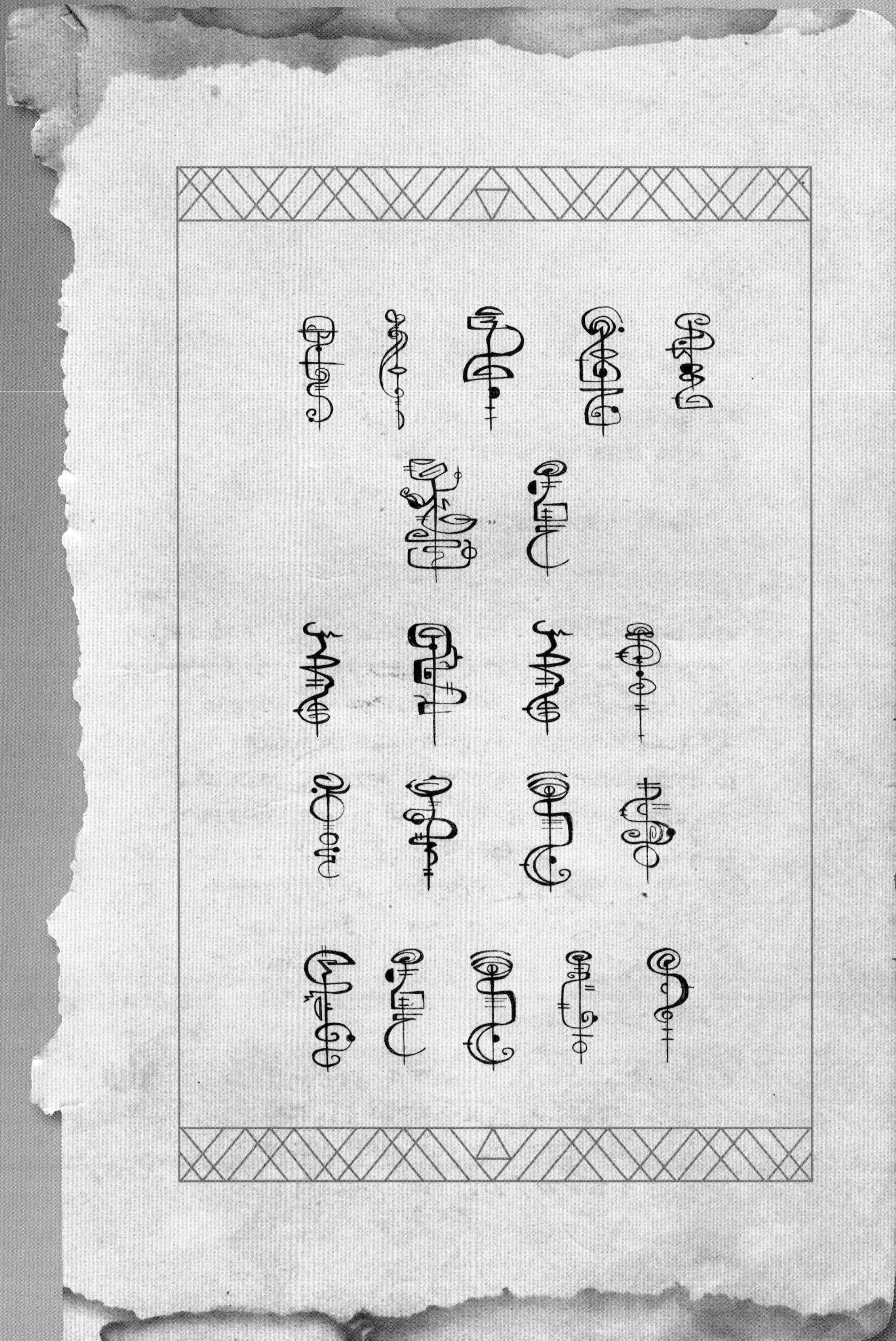

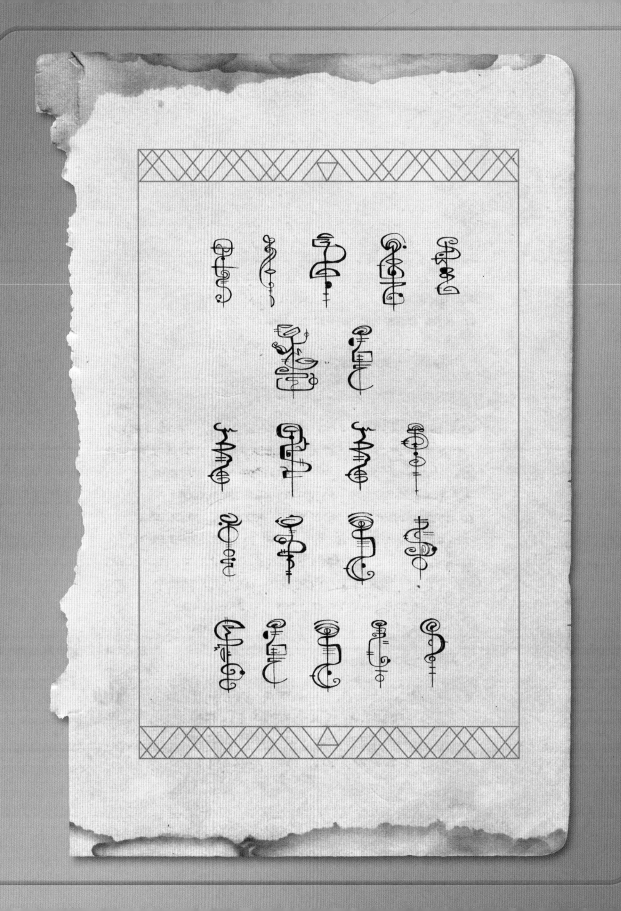

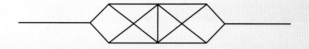

EXCERPT FROM *VULCANA'S BETRAYAL*

TRANSLATED FROM THE VULCAN

. . . Vulcana, once our beloved protector, has now abandoned us, and so we reject her. The words of the Dissembler have filled her ears, she believes his lies, and feeds them to her children. We are the only true ones left, but we cannot hold, we must leave for even we fear the lies of the Dissembler who has the power to take our young from us, and thus end us in time. Our seers have found our haven, in Death's Eye will we hide, build our Raptor's Nest and in time we—the warriors of the Raptor's Wing—will return and save Vulcana from her madness.

REPORT STATUS: 100745

MEMO

DATE: 20.9.59
TO: MEMBERS, UNITED EARTH COUNCIL
FROM: DOUGLAS, C-IN-C

RE: LOCATION OF ROMULUS

We have received intelligence from Vulcan detailing the origins of the Romulans. They are a splinter group from Vulcan who left the planet in the ancient past to start their own civilization, and the Vulcans have provided us with its location. This planet's location lines up nicely with what we know of Romulan fleet movements, and had already been one of our primary candidates for the Romulan homeworld.

This information is disturbing in that we also know that the Romulans may look very much like the Vulcans, and in fact may be indistinguishable from them with Human eyes. This has very serious ramifications, including the possibility of Romulans presenting themselves as Vulcans. There is likely a Romulan spy network already on Vulcan, which would explain the knowledge the enemy had of our security precautions on Starbase 1, as well as their knowledge (fortunately somewhat out of date) of defenses in the Sol system. Recommend we cut off all communication with the Vulcan government regarding our strategic decisions, and that we (quietly) step up our observations of any Vulcan movements at or near secure installations.

Of equal concern is the effect this knowledge will have on Earth's population. The Starfleet Information Service has done a commendable job in educating the public on the dangers of the enemy. Public fear and hatred for the Romulans is at a fever pitch, which frankly helps in the sacrifices we ask of the people of Earth in our war efforts. It would seem that the introduction of the revelation to the general public that Romulans are Vulcans would permanently destroy relations with our oldest ally in the Galaxy, and it would be the recommendation of this office that the information be kept top secret.

battle turned, and the two Romulan ships Tal left behind were easily defeated by *Enterprise* and *Atlantis*.

"We had fought a war from the position of underdog," Archer said. "The Romulans weren't used to being on an equal footing. They folded completely." Once the Romulan ships were destroyed, the two Starfleet ships then proceeded to destroy the shipyards.

And the defeat was even more humiliating than the one at Sol. Romulus was not yet under attack when Gileus had recalled his ships. Gileus had panicked when the Federation ship and its Denobulan companions were detected. The Romulan military maintained that if Gileus hadn't panicked and instead let the heavy cruisers stay engaged at Cheron, the Earth fleet would have been destroyed and the defensive systems around Romulus would have protected the planet long enough for reinforcements to arrive.

But Gileus didn't want to take that risk; in this critical moment, his focus hadn't been to win the war, but rather to protect his own power, which would have been threatened if Romulus were attacked. As soon as he realized the *Lexington*

LEFT: T'Pau, once a revolutionary, would eventually become one of Vulcan's most influential leaders. **OPPOSITE:** Memo from Admiral Douglas to the United Earth Council regarding the location of Romulus. He showed enormous foresight in his recommendation to the Council to keep the source of the information concealed. It was a debt the Vulcans would eventually repay. **FOLLOWING SPREAD:** The minute-to-minute recounting of the Battle of Cheron combines information from orbital observatories, ships' logs from both sides, and eyewitness accounts. Time logs are based on the internal ship chronometers of the Starfleet vessels.

06:37—Starships *Defiant*, *Enterprise*, and *Atlantis* come out of warp into the Cheron system. Admiral Gardner, aboard *Defiant*, is in command of the task force. *Defiant* and *Atlantis* attack defense satellites around Cheron, as *Enterprise* moves in to attack the orbital shipyard.

06:49—*Defiant* and *Atlantis* disable orbital defense satellites around Cheron. *Enterprise* engaged in battle with small support craft surrounding shipyard. *Defiant* and *Atlantis* move to assist *Enterprise*.

07:12—Seven Romulan ships, the warbirds *Chula*, *Apnex*, *Gal'Gathong*, *Rateg*, *Pensho*, *Koto*, and the flagship *ch'Rihan*, come out of warp in the Cheron system. *Defiant*, *Enterprise*, and *Atlantis* break off their attack on the shipyard, and move to engage the Romulan fleet.

07:15—The flagship *ch'Rihan*, under command of Admiral Tal, holds a position .5 AU from Cheron to coordinate the attack. *Chula* and *Gal'Gathong* go after *Defiant*; *Apnex* and *Rateg* go after *Enterprise*; and *Koto* and *Pensho* target *Atlantis*.

07:18—Admiral Gardner, aboard *Defiant*, orders the three ships to stay in tight formation into the atmosphere of Cheron. The Romulan ships pursue.

07:23—In the ionization layer of Cheron, *Defiant* leaves *Enterprise* and *Atlantis* and returns into orbit.

07:25—Once they pass through the layer, seeing that *Defiant* is gone, *Chula* and *Gal'Gathong* change course, returning to orbit to pursue *Defiant*.

07:27—*Enterprise* and *Atlantis*, more maneuverable in an atmosphere than the larger Romulan ships, turn upon their pursuers and inflict damage.

07:34—*Defiant* returns to the Cheron shipyards, using the superstructures of the drydocks as cover as *Chula* and *Gal'Gathong* press their attack.

07:39—Receiving reports that the Earth ships have the advantage in the atmosphere, Tal orders the four ships in the atmosphere to return to space and concentrate their fire on *Defiant*.

07:45—As the four Romulan ships turn to leave the atmosphere, *Enterprise* and *Atlantis* concentrate their fire upon *Apnex*, the rearmost ship, and disable its engines.

07:51—*Apnex* crashes on the surface of Cheron.

07:51—*Enterprise* and *Atlantis* take a low orbit course to come upon the shipyards from the opposite side. Admiral Tal, aboard *ch'Rihan*, loses sight of these two ships.

07:53—*Rateg*, *Koto*, and *Pensho* join *Chula* and *Gal'Gathong* as they attack *Defiant*. Losing maneuverability, *Defiant* concentrates its fire on one ship, *Pensho*. Gardner sends a coded message to *Enterprise* and *Atlantis* with the coordinates of *Pensho*.

08:03—*Enterprise* and *Atlantis* come up out of low orbit and also attack *Pensho*, destroying it.

08:07—*Defiant* is destroyed. All hands are lost with the ship.

08:09—With Gardner dead, Archer takes command of the remaining task force, and orders *Atlantis* to follow *Enterprise* and head toward the Cheron sun, with the hope that the star's gravity well will interfere with the Romulan targeting sensors. The remaining Romulan ships follow.

08:09—Admiral Tal receives orders directly from the Romulan praetor. Earth ships are moving to Romulus, Tal is to bring at least three ships back to defend his homeworld. Tal does not inform his praetor that he has already lost two ships, and follows orders.

08:10—Tal orders *Rateg* and *Gal'Gathong* to rendezvous with *ch'Rihan*. Tal orders Commander Byrn of the *Koto* to stay with *Chula* and continue to pursue and destroy *Enterprise* and *Atlantis*.

08:12—*Rateg* and *Gal'Gathong* follow *ch'Rihan* to warp out of the system.

08:13—Archer orders *Enterprise* and *Atlantis* to come about and attack the Romulan ships.

08:15—Byrn orders *Chula* to split off from *Koto*, in the hopes of taking one Earth ship with him.

08:16—Archer orders *Atlantis* to stay with *Enterprise*, and the two ships concentrate fire on *Chula*'s port engine. Byrn orders *Koto* back just as *Chula* loses its port engine.

08:17—*Koto* returns, but *Chula* can't maneuver, and *Enterprise* and *Atlantis* move out of *Chula*'s weapons range.

08:18—08:31—*Enterprise* and *Atlantis* engage in battle with *Koto*, and destroy it. They then move toward the Cheron orbital shipyards and destroy them.

08:37—*Enterprise* and *Atlantis* order *Chula* to surrender. Byrn refuses, and orders his ship to self-destruct.

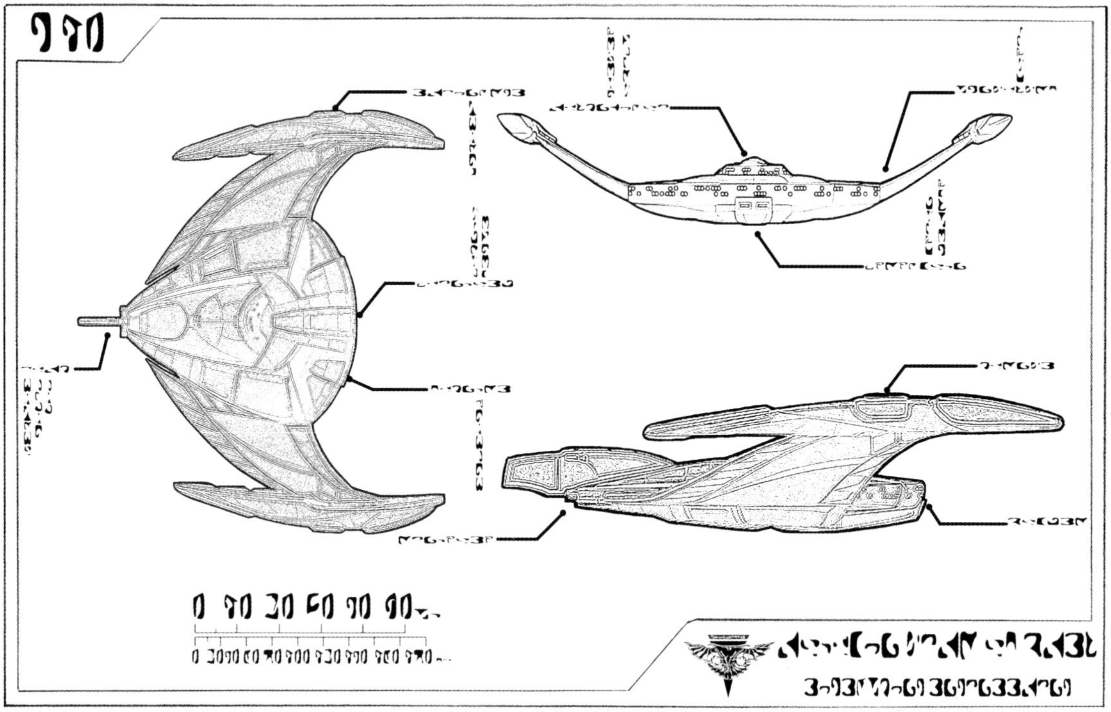

and the Denobulan ships would reach Romulus a day ahead of the ships he'd recalled from Cheron, he contacted Earth by subspace radio and suggested they begin negotiations for a peace to end this conflict. The Romulan War was over.

THE NEUTRAL ZONE

The United Earth Council found Gileus's message unexpected, but they didn't waste time. "It was clear to me that Gileus's suing for peace was in fact a surrender," Samuels wrote in his memoirs. Nathan Samuels dictated the terms. There would no longer be an ill-defined Romulan Empire border; Samuels instead established a neutral zone, where entry by either side would be considered an act of war.

"Though the penalty seemed equal to both sides," Samuels wrote, "in fact, I had succeeded in cutting off the Romulans from the rest of the Galaxy." He had made Earth the savior of the Alpha Quadrant; the Coalition planets, because of Earth's victory, were now protected from the Romulans. It was leverage that Samuels needed not only to rehabilitate his much damaged reputation, but also to close the loophole that had left Earth alone to face the Romulans to begin with.

ABOVE: A Romulan warbird, circa 2150. **OPPOSITE PAGE:** This excerpt from the Romulan/Earth peace treaty takes away territory Romulus had acquired during the war, and more specifically establishes the terms of the Neutral Zone, the borders of which would not be violated by either side for over a century.

TREATY OF PEACE BETWEEN ROMULUS AND EARTH

PEACE

ARTICLE 1

(A) THE STATE OF WAR BETWEEN ROMULUS AND EARTH IS TERMINATED AS FROM THE DATE ON WHICH THE PRESENT TREATY COMES INTO FORCE BETWEEN ROMULUS AND EARTH CONCERNED AS PROVIDED FOR IN ARTICLE 23.

(B) EARTH RECOGNIZES THE FULL SOVEREIGNTY OF THE ROMULAN PEOPLE OVER ROMULUS AND ITS TERRITORIAL SPACE.

TERRITORY

ARTICLE 2

(A) ROMULUS RECOGNIZES THE INDEPENDENCE OF DENOBULA, RENOUNCES ALL RIGHTS, TITLE, AND CLAIM TO DENOBULA.

(B) ROMULUS RENOUNCES ALL RIGHTS, TITLE, AND CLAIM TO ALGERON.

(C) ROMULUS RENOUNCES ALL RIGHTS, TITLE, AND CLAIM TO GALORNDAN CORE.

(D) ROMULUS AND EARTH RENOUNCE ALL RIGHTS AND CLAIM TO ANY SPATIAL BODIES DISCOVERED WITHIN THE SPACE DEFINED IN APPENDIX A AS "THE NEUTRAL ZONE." FURTHER, ROMULUS AND EARTH AGREE THAT VIOLATION OF THE BORDERS OF THE AREA DEFINED AS THE NEUTRAL ZONE WILL BE CONSIDERED AN ABROGATION OF THIS AGREEMENT.

CHAPTER III

THE FEDERATION

2160–2245

"Ex astris, scientia."
(From the stars, knowledge.)

—Starfleet Academy motto

OPPOSITE: Jonathan Archer speaking at the signing of the Federation Charter. Behind him, left to right, are Ambassadors T'Jan of Vulcan, Gort Sarahd of Andoria, Admiral Douglas, and Ambassador Natha Kell of Tellar.

The Romulan War had raised Earth's stature in the Galaxy to heroic proportions, giving the Humans political capital that they intended to spend. Unfortunately, it had also been very costly in lives and resources. Nathan Samuels and the United Earth Council knew that despite their success in the war, they were also vulnerable. They could not afford another intergalactic conflict, so every effort needed to be made to protect Earth. The Neutral Zone would be monitored by seven outposts constructed on asteroids. The Starfleet Corps of Engineers would bury the control centers of the monitoring outposts a mile deep in those asteroids and cover the asteroids themselves with a protective shell of castrodinium.

"I was confident there would be no more surprise attacks from the Romulans," Samuels wrote in his memoirs, "but now I was worried that somebody, the Klingons perhaps, might take advantage of Earth's weakened condition. I needed a bold move, a show of strength." To this end he called a second convention of the Coalition of Planets to amend the charter—to get what he'd wanted from the charter to begin with.

THE SECOND CHARTER CONVENTION

Samuels and Ambassador to the Coalition Thomas Vanderbilt agreed that getting the Coalition to approve a second charter convention would be the easy part. It required only a majority vote of the member delegates. With the exception of the Andorians and the Tellarites, the Coalition planets followed Vulcan's lead. Although Vulcan had lobbied to keep the Coalition from becoming any kind of military alliance, the war had changed their point of view significantly. T'Jan, now the Vulcan ambassador to Earth, recognized along with her government that they owed Earth a huge debt.

"It is my judgment," T'Jan wrote to her superiors, "that the fact that Earth kept the connection between our people and the Romulans a secret has saved us much future conflict." Indeed, the Vulcans would have found themselves pariahs in the Galaxy if the truth had been known.

"As illogical as it might seem, we owe them a debt," T'Jan continued, "one which we can repay by supporting their goals." Her superiors agreed with her, and as a result, T'Jan worked with Vanderbilt to gain the necessary votes to call the convention.

The more difficult challenge was amending the charter, which required a two-thirds vote of the delegates. Vanderbilt and T'Jan both agreed that, in order to amend the charter, Andoria's and Tellar's approval would be crucial. The smaller planets would be hesitant to join a military alliance given the devastation brought by the recent war unless they were certain that all the major powers in the sector were behind it. "I was confident in my abilities to negotiate with our allies," Vanderbilt said in an interview for *First Captain: A Biography of Jonathan Archer*, "but I knew there really was only one Human being who could guarantee Andoria's and Tellar's support: Jonathan Archer." Samuels agreed with him, and used the power of the United Earth Council to bring Archer home.

When Jonathan Archer received his final orders, to return *Enterprise* to Earth for decommissioning, he was surprised. "*Enterprise* was ten years old; it had been officially refitted twice and received a lot of upgrades," Archer said in *First*

Captain. "I felt it still had a lot of good years left in space." He had heard a new class of starship was about to make its debut, but that didn't seem to necessitate *Enterprise*'s retirement. It was only when he was contacted by Samuels himself that he learned the full story.

When Samuels told Archer his plan was to get the Coalition Charter amended, Archer immediately agreed to help. "I lost a lot of friends in the [Romulan] war," he said, "and knew that if the Coalition had stood with Earth the war would have been over a lot sooner. In fact, I think the alliance could have even prevented the war from happening at all."

Although Archer was glad to assist with the charter, Samuels recalled in his memoirs that Archer was less understanding of *Enterprise*'s retirement. "I explained to him," Samuels said, "that *Enterprise* had become a symbol. Our first Warp 5 ship had survived the war intact; it showed the Galaxy that Humans were here to stay. And frankly, I didn't want to risk anything happening to it." Reluctantly, Archer followed his orders, and on January 18, 2161, *Enterprise* returned home, one week before the first day of the convention.

From the beginning of the convention, Archer was deeply involved. His introductory speech at the opening ceremonies in the new grand auditorium at United Earth Headquarters would be memorized by schoolchildren for centuries to come. Delegates from eighteen worlds filled the auditorium, and sat enraptured from his opening sentence: "Space, the final frontier." After weeks of negotiation, the charter was successfully amended. The Coalition would now be an alliance of worlds that would protect each other in times of conflict.

THE UNITED FEDERATION OF PLANETS

During the negotiations over the charter, Vanderbilt began to see the potential for an even greater opportunity. His vision would lead quickly to a cascade of events that would change history.

At one of the many bumps in the road during discussions, Vanderbilt found himself in a room with the delegates from Vulcan, Andoria, Tellar, and the Earth colony on Proxima Centauri.*

Natha Kell, the delegate from Tellar, didn't just want the military alliance to help defend the member planets, he also wanted help maintaining his world's fleet. Ambassador Sarahd of Andoria had the same motive, but certainly wasn't going to let Tellar get help building new ships from the Coalition.

Vanderbilt understood that both these worlds devoted many of their resources to maintaining their fleets and as a result, their homeworlds often faced shortages of food and other resources. And Vanderbilt knew that they still worried that one of their old adversaries, if given help with their military, might decide to move against them in the future.

But Vanderbilt saw a diplomatic compromise that could reshape the quadrant. "While I was listening to [Andorian Ambassador] Sarahd and [Tellarite Ambassador] Kell shouting at each other," Vanderbilt wrote in *The Founding*, his own

---

***AUTHOR'S NOTE:** The Proxima Colony, or Alpha Centauri as it was more colloquially known, had become a thriving world in the century since Zefram Cochrane had helped found, and then terraform, the planet. They peacefully declared their independence twenty years before the founding of the Coalition.

memoir on the Federation's origins, "I could see the fear in their eyes of what the others might do. That was what drove them, and me. I thought if all these world governments were folded into one body, no one world could make a move on its own. It would take the fear away."

And there would be huge advantages: resources could be equally distributed, diplomatic moves would be voted on, and all the fleets of these worlds would be under one command. It would provide the ultimate security. By limiting it to the most powerful worlds in the Coalition, combining their spheres of influence into one large territory, other governments could and would lobby to join. It was a truly visionary idea, and, "Once it was in my head," Vanderbilt wrote, "I couldn't let it go, even if it made me a laughingstock."

He brought the idea to Samuels. The men later recounted that at this meeting Samuels was initially reluctant. "In my experience as a politician," Samuels told Vanderbilt, "when someone tries to convince you to share power, it generally means giving up power." But he had called this second convention to provide security for Earth, and Vanderbilt's proposal would provide this security much more efficiently.

"The one thing I did know was that I was constantly surprised how cooperative these governments had become," Samuels said, "and if there was ever a moment for Earth to try to make this happen, it was then." He brought the proposal to the United Earth Council, which gave the go-ahead for Vanderbilt to bring it to the other four governments.

Andoria and Tellar, although protective of their own power, were tantalized by the idea of what this collaboration would bring them. They were aware of the richness of

BELOW: Office of the President of the Federation, Paris, France.

resources available to Earth and Vulcan. Although these resources were available through trade, this agreement would mean much more. Their people would be provided for.

Vulcan, meanwhile, longed for more influence over violent species in the Coalition and this was one logical way to guarantee it. As Humans, the people of Proxima were the easiest to convince. All agreed that as long as the cultures of their individual worlds remained sovereign, they were on board.

Vanderbilt saw he had the votes. He faced now a logistical problem. "How do you write an intergalactic Constitution? I'd never done it before," Vanderbilt wrote in his memoir. "I'm not sure anybody had." Vanderbilt instructed his staff to work with the staffs of the other four member planets to cobble a document together.

They used as templates the Coalition Charter and the United Earth Constitution, as well as the governing documents of the member worlds. Where they found agreement was in an equal, democratic body with a president appointed to rule for a defined term. There would also be a military/exploratory arm, a judicial system, and a science council. Though it took months to hammer out, there was little conflict along the way.

"It didn't seem to take as long as I thought it would," Vanderbilt said. "My impression was that everyone really wanted this to work. Whatever we might have been afraid of before, the war with the Romulans had made our other fears less important."

The question came up mid-negotiation: what to call this new organization? Vanderbilt has been given credit for the name "United Federation of Planets," but recently unsealed logs call the origin of this name into question, as Jonathan Archer's captain's log mentions the name years before the organization's inception.* Since this has never been fully explained, the credit stays with Vanderbilt.

On October 11, 2161, the Constitution was signed in San Francisco by Ambassador Thomas Vanderbilt of Earth, Ambassador T'Jan of Vulcan, Ambassador Natha Kell of Tellar, Ambassador Gort Sarahd of Andoria, and Ambassador Titus Oleet for Proxima. It was Ambassador Kell who put the finest point on it. "We defy anyone, even the Romulans, to test our resolve now for collective security."

The Council's first act was to elect a president, and they unanimously elected Vanderbilt. Samuels was openly disappointed. He wrote in his unpublished memoirs, "I had wanted to make history, but history got away from me."

STARFLEET AND ITS ACADEMY

The Constitution for the United Federation of Planets provided for a unified fleet under the command of the Federation Council. The makeup of that organization would be similar to the Council; representatives from all the worlds would play a role and have an equal say. But the member worlds agreed that the fleet needed a chain of command.

"This had a double purpose," Vanderbilt remembered in his memoir. "The member worlds all had militaries, so a military structure was one they would respect. This would be necessary to keep the peace." The Federation's fleet would not be used to impose the Federation on other worlds; rather,

***AUTHOR'S NOTE:** Archer's defenders consider this at least circumstantial evidence that a Temporal Cold War did—or will—occur.

ARTICLES OF FEDERATION

PREAMBLE

WE THE BEINGS of Earth, Proxima Centauri, Vulcan, Andoria, and Tellar are resolved that henceforth our relations shall be those of worlds which, as sovereign equals, cooperate in friendly association to promote their common welfare and to maintain intergalactic peace and security, and are therefore desirous of concluding a union of their societies;

FOR WE HAVE AGREED that our worlds hold these truths to be self-evident: that all species are created equal; that their citizens are endowed with certain incontrovertible rights, protected by their societies; that among these rights are life, liberty, and the pursuit of those states-of-being each individual society holds in greatest esteem;

THE RECENT CONFLICT has proven a threat to these rights, and we have recognized that only in sharing the power of our societies can we guarantee the blessings of liberty to our posterity and ourselves.

IT IS THAT GOAL and those that follow that has led us to adopt these Articles of Federation to form a more perfect union, establish justice, ensure domestic and intergalactic tranquility, provide for the common defense, and promote the general welfare.

it was to be an instrument of civilization. The fleet would regulate commerce and use force only when necessary to protect its members. Its chief goal would be exploration; representing the Federation to new life and new worlds as the peaceful organization it set out to be.

The Andorians, Tellarites, and Vulcans did not see themselves—or one another—as the natural leaders of this kind of endeavor, and, still in awe of Earth's conduct during the Romulan War, turned to their Human colleagues to carry this out. In a previous time, the Vulcans had been wary of Earth outpacing them, but now they were ready to step in line behind the Earthlings who had more than proven themselves. Add to that, the goals were in many ways the same established goals of the Earth Starfleet. Thus, it was easily agreed upon by the newly formed Federation Council that the combined service mandated by the Constitution would be built under the Earth Starfleet's framework, and for continuity it would still be called "Starfleet Command."

Admiral Douglas, after his extraordinary service during the Romulan War, was offered the rank of commander-in-chief of Starfleet but turned it down. He had another project on the horizon.

"The biggest problem I faced during the war," Douglas is quoted as saying in the official Starfleet history of Starfleet Academy, "was the lack of well-trained crews." Not just crews who knew how to operate a ship, but ones who understood the Galaxy. "There was always such an influx of data," Douglas said, "it was near impossible for someone raised on a farm in Kansas to be ready to fight a battle in space. We lost a lot of men and women because we had to send them out unprepared."

When Admiral Douglas became aware that Starfleet would be part of the new Federation, he convened a meeting with representatives of the Federation's founding members' military organizations. The representatives agreed that the combined Federation Starfleet would also require combined training. A few months after the Constitution was signed, Douglas and officers from the Andorian Imperial Guard and the Tellarite and Vulcan fleets presented a proposal for an academic institution for Starfleet that would feature a curriculum contributed to by all the worlds of the Federation.

Starfleet Academy was approved and founded on December 13, 2161. Admiral Douglas would be its first commandant. "There was an opportunity here," Douglas said, "to fill our ships with well-educated, progressive individuals representing the Federation. People who weren't in the Federation would know us through the people in Starfleet. We had to put our best foot forward."

He solicited help not only from the Federation members' military organizations, but from their academic institutions as well. Starfleet Academy very quickly became one of the finest institutions for learning in the Galaxy. The Academy was built near Starfleet Headquarters in San Francisco. On September 8, 2166, Admiral Douglas delivered his commencement address to its first class of students.

Starfleet Command, meanwhile, was not waiting for these students to graduate. Once the Constitution was ratified,

OPPOSITE: The preamble to the Federation Constitution, more formally known as the Articles of Federation. The preamble has echoes of the Tribunal of Alpha III, the United States Constitution, and the United States Declaration of Independence.

no time was wasted putting the combined resources of the worlds of the Federation to work. The shipyard on Utopia Planitia received an influx of alien expertise and technology, and the Warp 7 ships that had been slowly coming together came off the assembly line at a breakneck pace. By mid-2162 five Warp 7 ships, called the *Daedalus* class, were exploring the Galaxy in the name of Starfleet: the United Space Ship (*U.S.S.*) *Daedalus*, *Essex*, *Horizon*, *Valiant*, and *Archon*. Though they would have their successes, the *Daedalus*-class vessels would be marked by tragedy.

FIRST FLEETS

The Starbase program also flourished. Although at the end of the Romulan War there were only three completed Starbases, by the mid-2160s there were fifteen spread across the Alpha Quadrant. During this period, the Starbases, as well as the outposts along the Neutral Zone, came to define the borders of the Federation 500 light-years across.*

The *Daedalus*-class vessels bravely explored beyond that border, but not without losses. Within a decade of their launch, the *Essex*, the *Archon*, and the *Horizon* would be lost with all hands, and it would take a very long time to discover their respective fates (over a century for the *Archon* and *Horizon*, almost two for the *Essex*). The captain of *Essex* was Bryce Shumar, the sole survivor of the destruction of the *Excalibur*.

In later interviews, Admiral Douglas would say that the eagerness to complete the first five ships of the class was to blame. "We were in too big a hurry," Admiral Douglas said. "We filled those ships with the best people we had, but those first five ships had been rushed through the assembly line to get them ready for the war. When the war ended, we should've taken a little more time before sending them to the frontier."

Still, *Daedalus*-class vessels had some success in their explorations, making many scientific discoveries, which were brought back to the Federation Science Council, whose chief minister during this period was Eric Vebber.

"It was an amazing period," Vebber said in his book *Hodgkin's Law: How Termites Explained the Galaxy*. "I'd been a professor at the American Continent Institute when I was chosen to lead the Council. The *Daedalus* ships were sending us a treasure trove of scientific information, and it was my job to organize it and distribute it to the member worlds."

Of particular interest to Vebber and his team was the prevalence of Earth-like cultures and humanoid species throughout the Galaxy. "As a scientist, it seemed counter-intuitive," Vebber said in an interview. "Given the wide variety of life in the universe, why would the overwhelming majority of civilizations be populated by people who looked

OPPOSITE: In September of 2166, Admiral Douglas delivered the commencement speech to the first graduating class of Starfleet Academy. Note that this speech suggests the graduates take actions that would eventually be outlawed by the Prime Directive. Among the graduates of this class was James Ogaleesha Davis, maternal grandfather—and namesake—of James T. Kirk. ***AUTHOR'S NOTE:** Starbase 2 and 3 were completed in 2158, Starbase 4 was completed in 2160. Starbase 1 was abandoned by the Romulans as a condition of the peace and Algeron fell into the boundaries of the Neutral Zone. As a monument to all the lives that were lost in the destruction of Starbase 1, Starfleet "retired the number" and has never commissioned another starbase with the designation "1."

AD ASTRA PER ASPERA

Congratulations to you, my fellow officers, the first graduating class of Starfleet Academy. I could not be prouder to stand here on this day. A momentous day not just for this Academy, not just for Starfleet, but for the United Federation of Planets and the galaxy it inhabits. The demands that will be made upon you in the service of your government in the coming months and years will be more pressing, more burdensome, more challenging, and, I hope, more fulfilling than ever before in our history.

This institution was born out of war, a terrible conflict that cost the lives of our brothers and sisters and mothers and fathers. But if this institution is a success, then this class will help guarantee that war will no longer be the way of life for the people we represent.

There is no question that we have trained you to be soldiers, but never soldiers first. You are always something else first. Some of you are scientists, some educators, some healers, some engineers. The soldiers in all of you will sit in the shadow of your primary duties, hoping that they never are called. You leave here today to join your comrades in Starfleet as explorers, as peacemakers, as guardians of the citizenry of our worlds.

The problems you will face will be demanding. You will serve as advisers to beings you have no biological connection to, perhaps helping elevate primitive cultures to our level of prosperity. You will negotiate treaties with broad political and military ramifications. You will go to the far corners of space, hold delicate command posts out on the edge of civilization. The scope of your decisions will not be confined to any tradition we currently understand. You will need to learn new languages and understand new cultures and new systems of government. On many worlds, your posture and performance will provide the local population with the only evidence of what our union is really like. From the moment you leave this lawn and step out into space, you represent not just yourself, but all the worlds of the Federation. You are our ambassadors.

But remember, most important of all, because we are only mortal, that, once faced with the unknown and the dangers it may present, you may lose sight of your goals. We hope that this won't happen, but if it does, remember, we did not send you out there alone. You have each other; find the strength to ask for help.

Today, we leave here to meet our separate responsibilities. I will go back to my office, and make preparations for next year's curriculum. You will go to protect our unions' vital interest by peaceful means if possible, by resolute action if necessary. And we go forth confident of support and success because we know that we are working for each other and for all those beings in the Galaxy who are determined to be free.

Thank you, and good luck!

U.S.S. VALIANT
STARFLEET COMMAND

First Officer's Personal log, this is probably my last entry. I don't know if anyone is going to find this. I don't even know if it matters. If a Starfleet ship comes into orbit of Eminiar VII, it's a good as dead. They have heat beams that overwhelmed Valiant's defensive systems immediately. After that first hit, almost every panel on the bridge was exploding. The captain was dead. I sounded the evacuation code signal, and got to an escape pod. Four crew members made it with me, and when they hit us again. we got out. One of them, Ensign Fernandez. Jonathan... he died when we crashed. The other two, Lieutenants Friedman and Shiban, were captured trying to get us food yesterday. There's no way to rescue them. The Eminian security is the best I've ever seen, and their disruptor weapons are very deadly. Don't know what happened. The captain communicated with their ruling council, it seemed to be five, and then I don't know. I'm in the basement of some building in their capital city. They're going to find me. If this log does survive me, please

like us? There had to be an explanation." Vebber found the answer to this in the work of a twenty-first-century biologist, A. E. Hodgkin. In 2093, Hodgkin visited the planet Locarus Prime, where he discovered termites. Though one would have assumed that those termites were somehow transplanted from Earth, Hodgkin, after examining their DNA, linked them directly to the Loracus biosphere. Hodgkin began working on a theory, which eventually was called "Hodgkin's Theory of Parallel Planet Development." It eventually drew links from the primitive biological stages to societal developments, from family units to forms of government.

"I was always a fan of this theory," Vebber said, "but in his day, Hodgkin didn't have access to enough data to prove it. Suddenly, in my job as head of the Federation Science Council, I did." Vebber would prove Hodgkin's Theory, declaring it Hodgkin's Law of Parallel Planet Development, which received the approval of the Vulcan Science Academy.

"I wasn't a snob about the Vulcans," Vebber wrote. "That thrilled me to death."

BOLD BEGINNINGS

The work of these first Federation starships also served as a prelude to the coming decades. The *Daedalus*, commanded by Malcolm Reed (who had served as Archer's security chief for his entire career as a starship captain), was the first Starfleet vessel to visit the planet Organia. Reed and

ABOVE: Starfleet Academy, San Francisco, California. **OPPOSITE:** Though Starfleet ships went in peace, the dangers they faced were not to be underestimated, especially where first contact was concerned. The *Daedalus*-class *Valiant* (the second ship with that name to be lost in space) went to the Eminiar system with the intent to open diplomatic relations, but found itself in the middle of an interplanetary war. The *Valiant* was destroyed in orbit. A few crew members were able to evacuate the ship in an escape pod and land near one of the largest cities. They survived for a few days before being captured and executed. It would be another hundred years before the war ended, and Eminiar became a member of the Federation. It was then that the handwritten log from the last surviving crewman, Commander Lee Billings, was brought home.

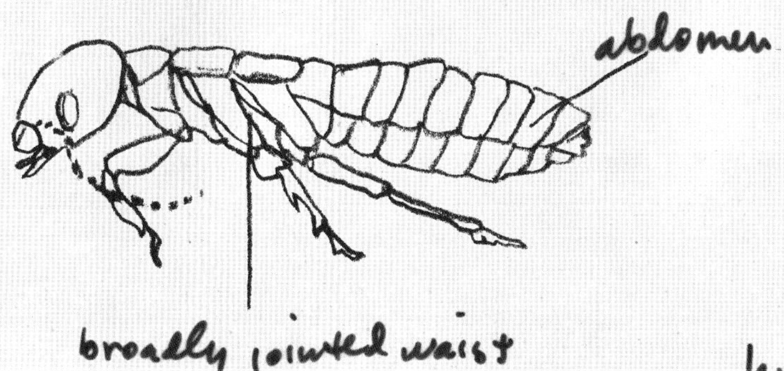

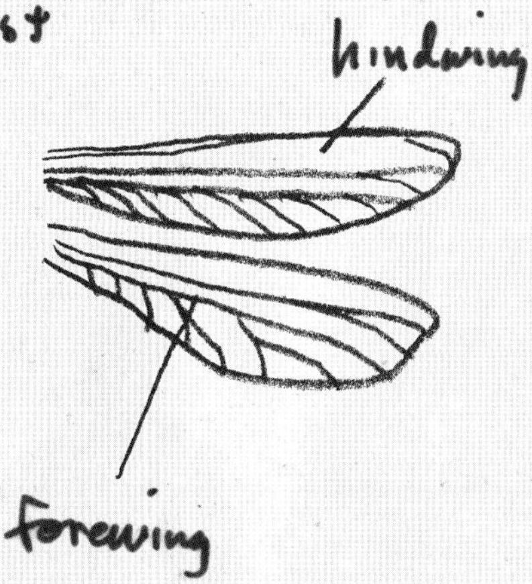

... so the termites of Loracus, with no genetic similarity to termites on Earth, nevertheless had the same type of society: they divided labor among castes, they produced overlapping generations and collectively took care of young.

Before I set out to theorize how this may have happened, it is an important development in that it implies that higher forms of life, were they to develop on other worlds, might also develop similar or even identical, civilizations. It has always seemed more likely that the opposite is true, that alien civilizations would be far from what we on Earth find familiar. Yet we already have the evidence of the Vulcans, who, aside from looking like us, had at least similar periods in their history that parallel events on Earth. Perhaps the termites of Loracus tell us this may not be the exception, but the rule...

his crew found a very primitive, peaceful culture but in Reed's captain's log he posted that he was surprised by the Organians' reaction to their visitors. He had expected the Organians to treat him and his crew as gods, and yet they seemed to have no reaction to them landing a shuttlepod in the middle of their town square. As the future would tell, the Organians were not at all primitive; they were in fact far more advanced than the Federation.

At this time, however, Reed had no idea of their true natures—and thought nothing of possibly contaminating what he believed was a primitive culture.

Before the *Horizon* was lost, Captain Vince Waldron had a similarly cavalier attitude. His ship visited the planet Sigma Iotia II, and the *Horizon*'s contamination of that culture would turn the entire planet into a replica of 1920s Chicago. (For more detailed information on this, see *A Piece of the Action: The Unique Case of Sigma Iotia II* by Edward Paskey.) Such bold entrances by starships and their captains on primitive worlds would soon become a thing of the past.

THE KLINGON QUESTION

Once established, the Federation found that its most consistent source of conflict was from the Klingon Empire. The Klingons were in an expansion mode as well, but fortunately they were not seeking territory currently governed by the Federation. However, contacts between Federation starships and Klingon vessels almost always were tense, if not outright hostile. It became clear that the Klingons viewed Starfleet, and particularly Earthlings, with distrust and disdain. The Federation, ultimately concerned with maintaining the peace, was finally spurred into action when the Starfleet vessel *Rochelle* was attacked by a Klingon warship while escorting a Denobulan freighter. The Klingons, claiming the ships were violating their territory, fired on them, destroying the freighter. One of Earth's oldest allies, Denobula had considered joining the Federation for many years. However, this act of hostility caused the Denobulans—already scarred from the Romulan War—to withdraw from galactic affairs.

The Klingons destroyed the Denobulan freighter because it was being escorted by what they called a "Human" ship. Starfleet and the Federation Council recognized that the Klingon hostility toward Earth was a developing problem that needed to be addressed. It was not only worrisome in the Klingons' interactions with Earth, but it was affecting the Klingon attitude toward the entire Federation. In 2174, the Federation commissioned a study by the Science Council to determine the root of this hostility.

OPPOSITE: Albert Elias Hodgkin was a unique biologist, the first to conclusively connect genetics to higher levels of societal structures. In this passage from his notebooks—published posthumously—he makes a leap that his data was still far from fully supporting. **FOLLOWING PAGES (104):** The captain's log excerpt is from the *S.S. Daedalus* on the first contact with the Organians. **(105):** The Prime Directive has become one of the key provisions in the Federation Charter. Its importance has been continually reinforced since its implementation. One case involved the planet Sigma Iotia II. The twenty-third-century *Starship Enterprise* revisited Sigma Iotia II and discovered the unique contamination caused by the initial encounter. The following report to the Federation Council addresses the way the Federation dealt with this planet, and attempted to correct the unintentional contamination.

Daedalus Captain's Log, June 13, 2165

We landed on Organia about an hour ago and I have to say everything that has happened since has been surprising. As we approached the largest village we could see people farming and using horse and wagons. Our shuttlepod landed in the middle of what looked like a village out of Medieval England. My helmsman, Georges Picard, and I stepped out of the ship, prepared to talk a primitive people out of considering us gods, but we were pretty much ignored by most of the populace, who simply went about their business.

An elderly man walked over to me and said, "you're early," and smiled at me as if in some private joke, and moved along. We tried to find some kind of ruling body, but there doesn't seem to be any. So we took our readings and gathered whatever information we could, and I guess we're going to leave. Not sure what else we're supposed to do.

To: Federation Council
From: Xander Cohen, Secretary for Planetary Affairs
Re: The Disposition of Sigma Iotia II

Summary:
In 2168 the *Daedalus*-class ship *Horizon* made first contact with Sigma Iotia II. Shortly after its visit to the planet, the ship was lost with all hands in an unsuccessful attempt to navigate the Mutara nebula. Before it was lost, the ship's subspace receiver was damaged, so the captain sent his ship's logs by conventional radio transmission. They were only received by Starfleet Command last year, on Stardate 4408.2, almost one hundred years after they'd been sent. A cursory examination of this ship's logs reveals that the captain and crew might have contaminated Sigma Iotia II's culture. The *U.S.S. Enterprise* was ordered to investigate.

Enterprise, under command of Captain James T. Kirk, discovered that the *Horizon* had caused a unique contamination: the entire planet seemed to have based their government and culture on a book called *Chicago Mobs of the Twenties*. The planet was made up of disparate "gangs," who fought for control over their territories.

For reasons detailed in Captain Kirk's log, he determined that uniting the planet under a "syndicate" of gangs and requiring it to be answerable to the Federation would reduce the chaos and bloodshed. Kirk intimidated the Iotians, requiring that this "syndicate" would "cut" the Federation in for forty percent of its profits, and that a Federation starship would return annually for this "cut."

Upon the orders from Starfleet, the *U.S.S. Defiant*, under command of Daniel Staley, returned to Sigma Iotia this week, and filed a report, excerpted below:

> ". . . we were greeted by Bela Oxmyx and Jojo Krako, who had been left in charge. They offered us alcoholic beverages, and admired our "heaters," then took us into a conference room where they opened a large attaché case inside of which were stacks of currency, approximately 31,243,000 dollars (the Iotians have adopted the currency of the twentieth-century United States). Oxmyx and Krako laughed conspiratorially, said that they had a "good year."

Staley took the currency to Starbase 12. The question now is, what do we do with it? The only place our "cut" has any worth is on Sigma Iotia II, so my proposal is as follows:

- Send a team of advisers to establish a small educational institution on the planet.
- Pay individual Iotians to take classes from the advisers. These Iotians, in exchange for the pay provided by our "cut," will be tasked with educating other Iotians on the benefits of democracy, social welfare, education, and the establishment of other institutions to try to guide the planet away from its current culture.
- So that the educational institution is accepted by the current Iotian society, I propose it be called something along the lines of "Cash College," and that its stated purpose be to make Iotians rich. As of right now, that is the only goal of individual members of this society.

If the Council does not accept this proposal, I would point out that we will be sending another starship back to that planet next year to get another cut, and since Staley reported that the Iotians were excited by new technologies they were developing, the cut might even be larger.

"It wasn't easy to get information on internal Klingon affairs," Vebber wrote in his introduction to the study, "and we did not think that Klingons would share openly any information with Humans. That is why Council members from other worlds, specifically the Andorians and Tellarites, gathered most of the information for this study."

The study's findings drew a straight line back to the first meeting of Humans and Klingons, and the High Council's report regarding Klaang's return to Qo'noS by the *Enterprise* NX-01. After an exhaustive presentation of the facts, the study was harsh in its conclusions:

"In summation, Captain Archer interceding to save Klaang's life rather than letting him die with honor forever colored the Klingon view of Humanity. As we have seen in this study, in the years since that first encounter, any positive role Earth played in Klingon affairs has been ignored or dismissed by Klingon society—the 'meddling' and 'dishonorable' nature of Humans is always emphasized."

The study would have a profound effect, most notably on Jonathan Archer himself. Having retired from Starfleet as an admiral in 2169, Archer had moved into the diplomatic service and became Earth's ambassador to Andoria, where he was serving when the report was published.

"I was flabbergasted," Archer told his biographer. "It was difficult to face that my initial instincts could've been so wrong. In my mind, the study cast a pall over my entire

BELOW: The destruction of the Denobulan freighter.

career." He was determined to do something about it. Archer gave up his ambassadorship, and the next year, using his influence and profile, became a representative on the Federation Council. He had only one goal in mind.

The Articles of Federation already had strong language protecting an individual world's right to conduct their internal affairs how they saw fit. The Federation above all else valued a world's right to self-determination, as long as it didn't infringe on the freedoms of other members.

Archer wanted to add an amendment to this clause. The Articles would guarantee that the Federation and its exploratory arm, Starfleet, would not interfere with the culture or internal politics of any world, member or non-member.

This provision did not have immediate support from the Council. Many of the members did not see the necessity of placing such a stringent restraint on their fleet. But Archer was determined. "I had spent a long time in space," Archer said, "and I had a lot of examples of advanced civilizations taking advantage of primitive ones. To me, the limitation of a law like this was a testimony to the height of our civilization."

Archer fought passionately for it on the council, and succeeded in changing many minds. In 2178, the Council amended the Federation Constitution to include Starfleet General Order 1, otherwise known as the Prime Directive. This one law would serve to define the non-interference philosophy of the Federation for centuries to come. Seven years later, due in no small part to this achievement, Jonathan Archer was elected president of the United Federation of Planets.

THE AGE OF EXPLORATION

In its first sixty years of existence, the Federation experienced a rare, extended period of peace. Many worlds sought membership, and it was only through a strenuous vetting process that a world's government could gain acceptance. Meanwhile, uninhabited worlds were discovered and peacefully settled. The Federation Council was kept abreast of the needs of its member worlds, and tasked Starfleet with fulfilling those needs. Colonies sprang up across the galaxy: Tarsus IV, Berengarius VII, Deneva, Marcus XII, Aldeberon, the irreverently named Planet Q, and dozens of others were established during this period, often in response to a specific need from the member worlds. The mining colony on Janus VI was established in the late twenty-second century to provide pergium, the rare element used to power life-support reactors in artificial environments.

Not every colony was established out of functionality; the Federation was committed to the freedom of its people, allowing individuals to move freely within its borders. Individual colleges and universities, such as the American Continent Institute, funded their own exploration and survey missions. In 2170, a group of Native Americans left Earth and eventually settled on Dorvan V, where the colonists were completely devoted to preserving their cultural identity. It exists and flourishes to this day.

Often called the Age of Exploration, this was a period of unprecedented advancement and enrichment, the result of an efficient sharing of knowledge through exploration. The Federation Science Council found an uninhabited planetoid to establish a repository of all the knowledge gathered by Starfleet. Called Memory Alpha, it became the library of

Starfleet Command
General Orders and Regulations

GENERAL ORDER 1

SECTION 1:

Starfleet crew will obey the following with any civilization that has not achieved a commensurate level of technological and/or societal development as described in Appendix 1.

a) No identification of self or mission.
b) No interference with the social, cultural, or technological development of said planet.
c) No references to space, other worlds, or advanced civilizations.
d) The exception to this is if said society has already been exposed to the concepts listed herein. However, in that instance, section 2 applies.

SECTION 2:

If said species has achieved the commensurate level of technological and/or societal development as described in Appendix 1, or has been exposed to the concepts listed in section 1, no Starfleet crew person will engage with said society or species without first gathering extensive information on the specific traditions, laws, and culture of that species civilization. Then Starfleet crew will obey the following.

a) If engaged with diplomatic relations with said culture, will stay within the confines of said culture's restrictions.
b) No interference with the social development of said planet.

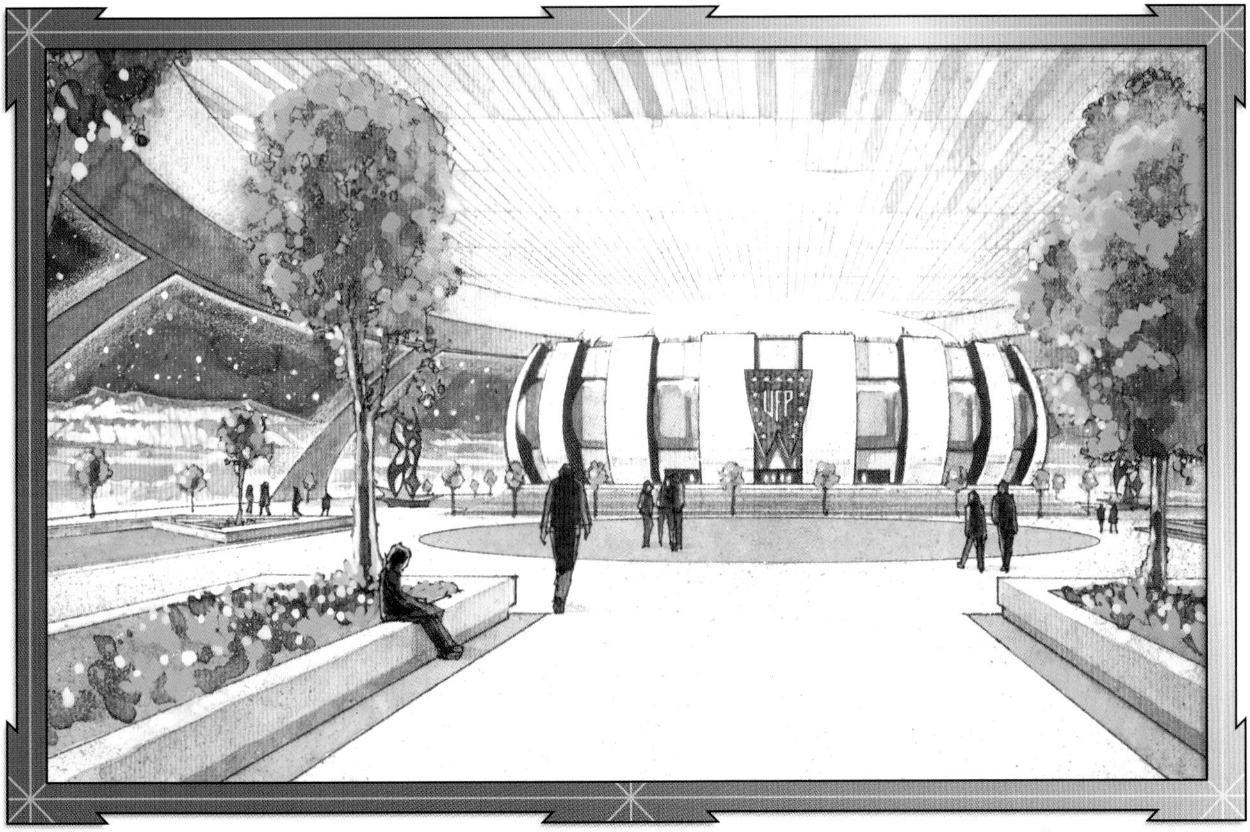

the Federation, where academics from across the quadrant could come to receive the up-to-date information on every field of scientific study, and examine original source material that cannot be reproduced.

By 2196, when the *Daedalus*-class vessels were removed from service and replaced by the new *Einstein* and *Baton Rouge* classes, Starfleet was now almost completely crewed by graduates of the Academy. For thirty years these graduates—the Galaxy's best and brightest—explored and catalogued the universe, sending information back to Starfleet Command computer technicians either on Earth or on the many starbases. These computer technicians updated the information in their computer cores, then sent subspace "packets" to every base, world, and ship in the fleet.

During this time, it also became clear that an Earth-based date system was not appropriate for a galaxy-wide organization. Thus, at the dawn of the twenty-third century, the Federation implemented the stardate system. Based on a mathematical equation affected by a vessel or world's location in the Galaxy, it was a standardization of

ABOVE: The main lobby of Memory Alpha. **OPPOSITE:** What was meant to be a simple rule of non-interference has grown into one of the most complicated laws in the Federation. Constructed to be a "living" document, by the twenty-fourth century the Prime Directive had forty-seven sub-orders. When it was first conceived, it had two main goals: to prevent misunderstandings between civilizations and to protect primitive worlds that were not ready to receive advanced technology.

time-keeping that favored no one planet. Individual worlds still kept their own calendars, but once in space, everybody had the same watch.

Starfleet and the Federation were helping civilization reach its pinnacle. But they were both about to face their greatest challenge.

2223: THE DILITHIUM CRESCENT

Though many sources of the valuable crystal dilithium—essential to the warp engines of the interstellar civilizations who used matter/anti-matter propulsion—had been discovered and developed over the centuries by many space-going species, it wasn't until the beginning of the twenty-third century that a Klingon scientist named Krent developed a theory as to where the greatest concentration of these resources were. He discovered that a unique combination of forces resulting from the formation of the Milky Way Galaxy had produced a stretch of space where dilithium was most likely to be found. This area, dubbed the Dilithium Crescent, became crucial to the Empire. The Klingons were the only people who had made this discovery; it gave them a very substantial edge when searching for new sources of the powerful element. When the discovery was initially brought before the Klingon High Council, it was decided that every effort needed to be made to keep it a secret, and the Klingons succeeded in this for several decades. (Krent was given the highest honor ever afforded a Klingon scientist: a state execution to keep his discovery quiet.)

Upon Krent's discovery, the mining ships of the Empire were ordered to concentrate their search efforts in the Dilithium Crescent. Although part of the area was already within the Klingons' sphere of influence, much of it wasn't. The Empire quickly sought to change that.

Sussman/MacFarlane, the main sequence star in the Crescent, had no Class-M planets ("M" stood for "*Minshara*," a Vulcan term adopted by Starfleet that referred to planets with oxygen/nitrogen atmospheres that could support humanoid life), but it did have a dense asteroid belt where the Federation mining ship *Castro* had staked a claim. The *Castro*'s captain, an asteroid prospector from Earth named Troy Adams, had only discovered minute traces of dilithium but took a gamble that there was more. He would never find out; on June 18, 2223, a Klingon D5 warship entered the system and destroyed the *Castro* without any warning. It then sent out a subspace transmission signaling that the system belonged to the Klingon Empire.

The problem for the Federation was that the Sussman/MacFarlane system (named for the two astronomers from Proxima who charted it) was not technically part of the Federation. Adams's claim on the system and his death created a delicate diplomatic issue. Ultimately, the Federation took the stance that though the system didn't belong to them, it wasn't Klingon either, and the Klingons had greatly overstepped by destroying a Federation ship and killing a Federation citizen.

It was clear that the Federation would not—nor could not—go to war over the death of a single person, but they had other avenues to pursue. Federation planets would no longer be allowed to trade with the Klingon Empire, and those non-Federation worlds who traded with the Klingons would find their contracts with the Federation under review. The Klingons, who had had a robust trade relationship with many worlds, suddenly found themselves cut off by these sanctions—not just in terms of dilithium, but also food and other resources.

The sanctions, however, only led to a more aggressive reaction from Qo'noS. Additional Klingon ships moved into systems they had not already laid claim to. This time, however, the Federation immediately disputed their territorial claims.

These tit-for-tat actions set the tone for Federation/Klingon relations for the next seventy years. They also played a role in the development of the most ambitious of Starfleet's ships.

CONSTITUTION CLASS

Robert April was a Starfleet officer who as an ensign served on an *Einstein*-class ship, the *Gates*, and later in his career had served as first officer aboard a *Baton Rouge*–class ship, the *Los Angeles*. His shipboard experiences and knowledge of Starfleet history had caused him to develop a sense of frustration at the limitations of the starships in service.

"We had to withdraw from our observation of the nova to return to Starbase 9 for just minor repairs," April wrote in a personal log while serving aboard the *Gates*, "repairs that could've been completed ourselves if the ship had been designed to be a little more self-sufficient."

April became increasingly convinced that a bolder step in starship design was needed. He envisioned a large ship manned by a crew in the hundreds—many of them scientists, provided with the latest research technology—with a sturdier design, and the ability to sustain a longer mission without contact with a repair base. The ship could also serve as the front line to defend the Federation, but its mission, like all Starfleet ships, would primarily be one of peace. After serving aboard the *Los Angeles* for three years, he requested a transfer to the Starfleet Logistics Command to pursue his dream.

April, an eclectic man with a love of science, had his own unique charisma. Once transferred to Starfleet Logistics, he rallied the department around him to pursue his project. He sought the help of a new generation of engineers and scientists to help him with his design. First, he wanted this ship to be fast. For decades, no Federation starship had been able to break the Warp 7 barrier. The Federation Science Academy had embraced the theory that it was in fact a time barrier and that exceeding Warp 7 would cause a ship to travel backward in time. None of the Federation adversaries had been able to break this barrier, so this point of view prevailed at Starfleet for decades. It ended with April.

"The only absolute proof that this was the final speed barrier," April said in his personal logs covering the development of the *Constitution*-class project, "was other people's failure to break it." He soon found the one engineer who agreed with him.

His name was Laurence Marvick, a young, brilliant engineer at the Cochrane Institute on Proxima, who had proposed a theoretical engine design that could exceed Warp 7. Not only was Marvick's engine design new—the computer that would control the reactor was also theoretical. No computer currently in use by Starfleet or anyone else was powerful enough to run Marvick's reactor. So April also needed to find someone to build a new computer.

Richard Daystrom, a twenty-four-year-old computer genius, had just won the Nobel Prize for a breakthrough in computer technology. Called Duotronics, it was the ultimate in both computational speed and user-friendly interface. Thinking that Daystrom might be able to help him, April sought him out. This turned out to be no easy feat.

"Daystrom wouldn't take my call," April said, "and why should he? He was being pursued by every major university and computer manufacturer in the quadrant." So April took the extraordinary step of beaming into Daystrom's office.

"I got a big black mark in my service record," April said, "but I also got to talk to Daystrom." The computer savant looked over Marvick's engine design, and was certain that a Duotronic computer would solve the problems. The Warp 8 engine was suddenly no longer impossible.

Although the ships themselves were designed to be more self-sufficient and operate for longer periods without repair, April proposed that the *Constitution*-class starships operate under five-year missions. This way, the starships could make use of the best minds in the Federation, including those who might not want to commit to a life of exploration. It would also allow the ships to be refitted with whatever technological breakthroughs had occurred during their time in deep space.

His design completed and practical, April made a proposal to Starfleet Command to commission twelve of the

BELOW: Left to right: Richard Daystrom, Laurence Marvick, and Robert April, with the finalized design for the *Constitution*-class ship.

ships. In turn, Starfleet took the plan to the Federation Council. "I knew I would need a campaign to get a project like this through the Council bureaucracy," April said, "so I built the campaign into the proposal."

According to his plan, every founding member of the Federation would make a contribution to the ships. Earth would design and build the superstructure; the Vulcans would provide the scientific sensors and equipment; the Andorians would provide the weapons and defensive systems; Tellar would provide the creature comforts of food and recreation technology; Proxima would design and build the warp engines. Each of these worlds would have a personal stake in a project that would provide their homeworld with its own production boon. The founding members would then subcontract to newer members, eventually making the program very attractive to every world in the Federation. April had envisioned this as a project that would go far beyond the initial twelve ships and this was how he would guarantee its longevity.

The project's approval, however, was stalled for a year with the Council. It was such a large undertaking that the details of it were combed through and argued many times. In the end, it was another threat to the Federation that precipitated the Council's full embrace of April's plan.

THE BATTLE OF DONATU V

Since the destruction of the *Castro* in 2223, the Asteroid Prospectors Association had sought Starfleet's protection. Starfleet was limited in terms of how many ships it could devote to this task, so to bolster its forces in the area near Klingon space (known simply as "the Disputed Area"), Starfleet put a few ships that had been retired back in service, including the re-fitted and re-armed *Patton* and *Eisenhower*—eighty-year-old *Marshall*-class light cruisers that had been part of the fleet that defended Sol during the Romulan War.

One of the systems in the Disputed Area, the star Donatu, had seven planets. None were capable of supporting humanoid life, but in 2242, a Federation survey of the fifth planet showed it was rich in dilithium; a prospecting station was set up. The Klingons sent three ships under the command of a Captain Klaar to remove the Federation prospectors. The Starfleet ships on patrol in that area picked up the Klingon task force and moved in to help the prospectors, but their crews knew they were no match for the Klingon ships.

The *Patton* was under the command of Lieutenant Commander Matthew Decker, a tough, aggressive officer. "I was a commander," Admiral Jose Mendez (ret.), the commanding officer of the *Eisenhower*, said in an interview with this author, "Matt Decker was only a lieutenant commander, so I had seniority. But Decker had an instinct about battle, so I took my lead from him."

Decker knew the Klingon ships could outgun the scouts, but the scouts had one advantage. The atmosphere of Donatu V was carbon dioxide and nitrogen, thick with clouds of sulfuric acid in a constant state of vigorous circulation.

"Decker told me to follow him out of warp near the planet," Mendez said, "and fire a volley of all our weapons. We would then drop into the atmosphere before the Klingons could get a bead on us." The Klingons were unprepared for this bold attack, and Decker and Mendez continued these hit-and-run tactics, popping out of the atmosphere, firing, and dropping back in. This allowed time for two

Baton Rouge–class ships to join them. By then, however, the Klingons had withdrawn.

The battle was considered inconclusive in determining the status of the area. However, its effect on the Federation Council was decisive: new ships suddenly seemed vital and April's plan was given a green light.

THE SECOND CONSTITUTION-CLASS STARSHIP

By 2243, April was overseeing the construction of the components of the first two ships in the San Francisco Navy Yards. The ships would be given the registry number Naval Construction Contract, or N.C.C., followed by a number. The first two: 1700 and 1701. It is interesting to note that the first ship out in space was *not* the first numbered: April took command of the second ship commissioned so he could stay in the development project a little longer. Command of the 1700 went to Garth of Izar, formerly captain of the *Baton Rouge*. Garth, an officer with a brilliant record, was also a perfectionist, and his obsession with detail slowed his ship's production process.

So in the end, it was April's ship that launched first, on April 11, 2245. In his captain's log from the day of the ship's launch, April jokingly denied that he planned the launch for the month of April—and also noted that there was only one guest at the launch whose presence he cared about, the former Starfleet captain whose ship's exploits had partially inspired April's project: Jonathan Archer. Archer, 133 years old, had lived long enough to see the launch of the first Starfleet ship since his own to be named *Enterprise*. April said that Archer had wished him luck before returning to his home in upstate New York. His era at an end, Jonathan Archer died peacefully the next day.

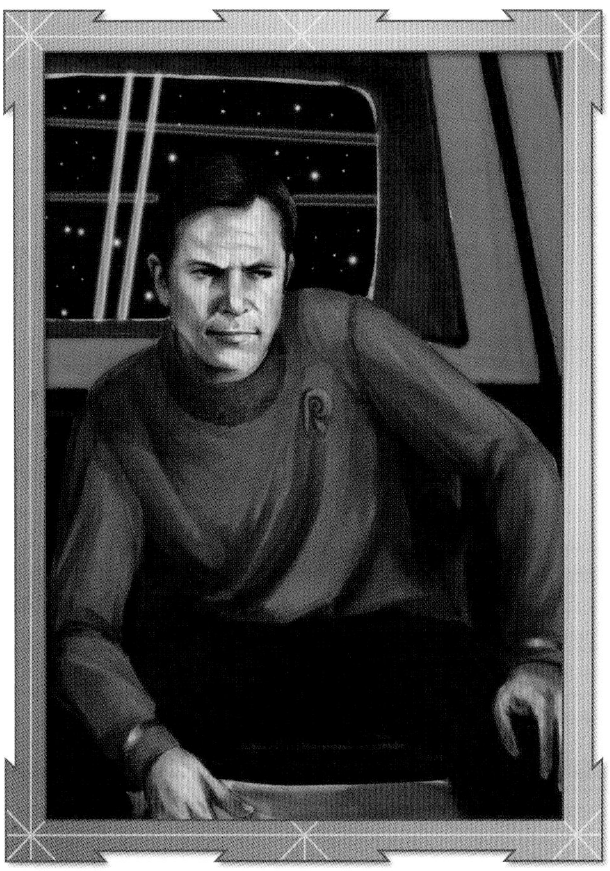

LEFT: Lieutenant Commander Matthew Decker of the *Patton*. He would eventually rise to the rank of commodore before his death in 2267. **OPPOSITE:** Robert April was commissioned as captain of the *U.S.S. Enterprise* on April 11, 2245. The commission harks back to the naval traditions of Earth that Starfleet still embraces to this day. **FOLLOWING SPREAD:** The Tellarites enforced very aggressive trade practices with anyone they went into business with, as illustrated in this trade agreement to mine pergium on Akaali. If examined closely, it appears that the Tellarites were not, in fact, agreeing to provide anything in exchange for the right to mine on the Akaali planet.

THE DELEGATES OF THE UNITED FEDERATION OF PLANETS
OF EARTH, ANDOR, VULCAN, TELLAR, AND PROXIMA CENTAURI TO

Robert April, Starfleet Officer

WITH THE RANK OF

Captain,

REPOSING SPECIAL TRUST AND CONFIDENCE IN YOUR
PATRIOTISM, VALOR, CONDUCT, AND FIDELITY,

★ ★

Do by these Presents, constitute and appoint you to be Captain of the *United Space Ship Enterprise*, Naval Construction Contract *One Thousand Seven Hundred and One*, in the service of Starfleet and the Council of the United Federation of Planets, fitted out for the exploration of the Galaxy, with the general missions to seek out new life and new civilizations, to regulate commerce, and in the defense of our liberty, and for repelling every hostile invasion thereof. You are therefore carefully and diligently to discharge the Duty of Captain by doing and performing all Manner of Things thereunto belonging. And we do strictly charge and require all Officers and Crew under your Command to be obedient to your Orders as Captain, and you are to observe and follow such Orders and Directions, as you shall receive from this or a future Council of the United Federation of Planets, or Commander-in-Chief of Starfleet Command, or any other superior Officer, according to the Rules and Disciplines of Starfleet, the Usage of Space, and the instructions herewith given you, in Pursuance of the Trust reposed in you. This Commission to continue in Force until revoked by this or a future Council or Starfleet Command.

San Francisco, April 11, 2245,

By Order of the Federation Council President, *Samuel Solomon Qasr*.

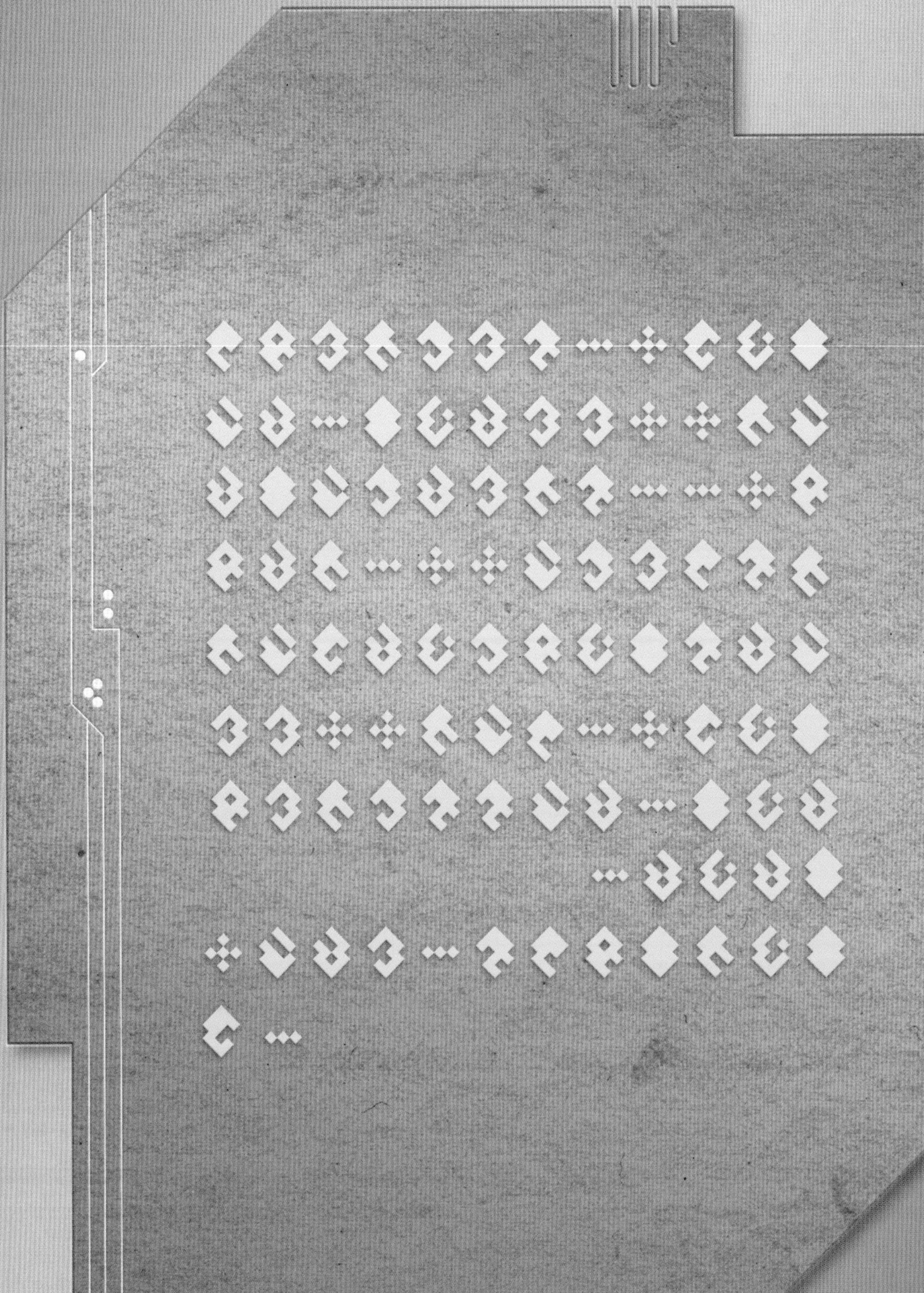

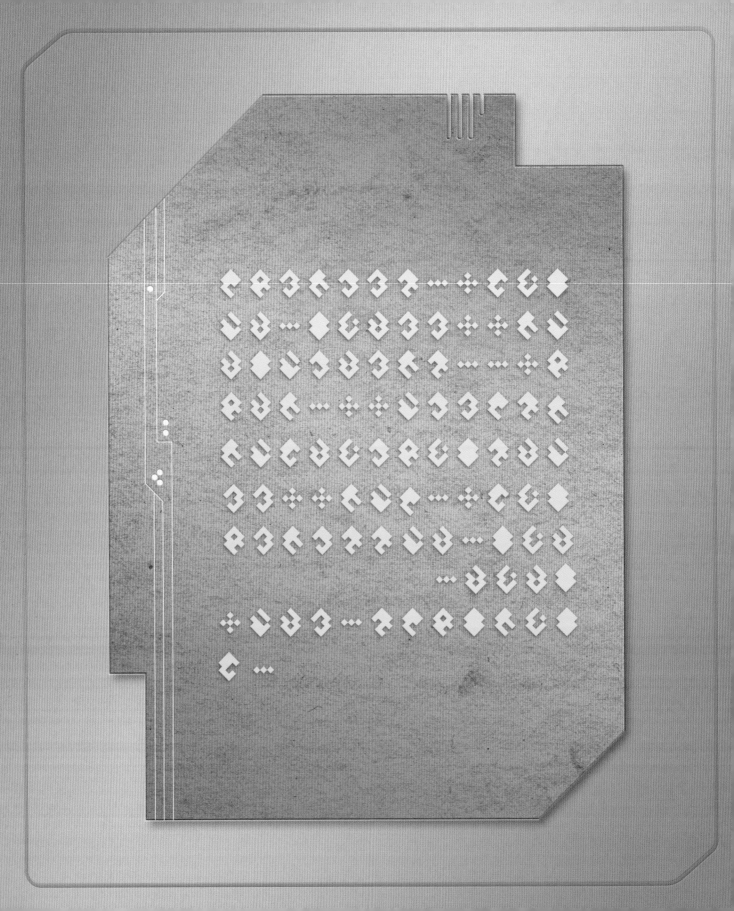

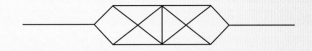

TRADE AGREEMENT BETWEEN TELLARITE MINING CONSORTIUM AND THE AKAALI GOVERNMENT

TRANSLATED FROM THE TELLARITE

1. The Akaali Government agrees to allow the Tellarite Mining Consortium to mine the element PERGIUM on the southern continent, coordinates latitude 34.045, longitude −118.521.

A) The Akaali agree that this agreement covers any source of pergium discovered during the term of this contract.

B) The Akaali agree that this agreement covers any source of any element that the Tellarite Mining Consortium discovers on the Akaali world during the term of this contract.

2. Tellarite Mining Consortium agrees to provide Government of Akaali with 20% of the gross income from the sale of the mined ore.

A) Akaali Government agrees that 20% of the gross income will go toward coverage of incidental expenses incurred during transportation off planet of the mined ore.

3. The Government of Akaali agrees to provide living facilities for Tellarite Miners and their families.

A) Akaali Government also agrees to provide food, unless:

I) food is indigestible to Tellarite physiology or,

II) food is unpleasant to Tellarite palate.

B) In the case of Section 3, Paragraph A, subsection I &/or II, the Akaali agree to reimburse Tellarite Mining Consortium for importation of appropriate food.

4. The length of term of this contract is limited to three years unless the Tellarite Mining Consortium informs the Government of Tandara that they intend to extend the term.

CHAPTER IV

THE EDGE OF NIGHT

2245–2290

"I'm starting to realize that 'we come in peace' only means something if they're clear on the fact that we can also kick their ass."

—Matthew Decker, Starfleet Commodore,
excerpt from his log, Stardate 4197.3

OPPOSITE: An artist's rendering of the Organian Ayelborne simultaneously appearing in the offices of the Federation president and the Klingon chancellor.

By 2250, the twelve *Constitution*-class ships were aloft, heading out in twelve different directions from Starfleet Command, to become the lead ships of Starfleet.

Enterprise had been given a patrol area that not only included the Neutral Zone with the Romulans, it also encompassed the Disputed Area with the Klingons. Eventually, this ship would face conflict on all fronts, but, ironically, one of its first missions would remind the Federation that not all enemies come from outside. It would also have a profound effect on the man who would become the most famous Starfleet officer of his day—and who would come to define this new era.

TARSUS IV

The Tarsus system, first mapped by the *Essex*, was at the edge of known space, on the other side of the Galaxy from the Romulans and the Klingons. The fourth planet was settled in the late twenty-second century by a group of Humans who sought a life away from conflict. Many were veterans of the Romulan War, accompanied by their families. They hoped that by removing themselves from Earth and its allies, they could live a more peaceful existence. Once the Tarsus IV government was established, it was accepted as part of the Federation. For many years, Tarsus IV was a self-sustaining and peaceful world.

Then, in 2246, an alien fungus entered the food chain of the planet and destroyed most of the food supply. The 8,000 inhabitants on Tarsus IV panicked. Kevin Reilly, later an officer in Starfleet, was born on Tarsus IV and was a child when the crisis occurred. He recorded his recollections for Memory Alpha as part of a living witness project on the Tarsus IV disaster: "I remember my parents locked the door to our house," Reilly said. "I overheard them talking about the fact that the food would be gone long before help could arrive." The government took a different turn.

Since its inception, Tarsus IV had been a technocracy. The decision-makers of the ruling council were scientists, engineers, and technicians who had been selected based upon how knowledgeable they were in their field. There was a governor-type figure named Kodos, who was appointed by the council based upon his managerial ability to deal with problems and delegate tasks, but he was not elected. Most of the colonists didn't even know what he looked like. Now, however, this governor was faced with a terrible crisis. And he was the wrong man at the wrong time.

OPPOSITE: During this period, many worlds sought admission to the Federation. It was a long and arduous process for them to prove that they had reached a level of civilization where they were able to operate within its laws. (In fact, many historians question whether the Tellarites and Andorians, had they not been founding members, would have been admitted today under the requirements they helped establish.) Federation members' homeworlds must be governed under a democracy. But admission to the Federation was not always an easily made decision, even among its own members, as was the case with the Coridan admission. Coridan was a world that had served as a pawn in intergalactic politics for over a century before it was finally admitted, and its people struggled for a long time to meet the requirement of democracy. The vote of the Federation Council was greatly influenced by the findings of the Babel Conference of 2268.

CORIDAN ADMISSION ACT OF 2268

On the recommendation of the Babel Conference of 2268 included herein, be it enacted by the Council of the United Federation of Planets assembled, that, subject to the provisions of this Act, and upon issuance of the proclamation by the President of the Council required by section 12d of this Act, the planet Coridan is hereby declared to be a member of the United Federation of Planets.

It is admitted into the Federation on an equal footing with the other worlds in all respects whatsoever, and the document formed pursuant to the provisions of the Act of the United Government of Coridan entitled, "An Act to provide for the holding of a convention to prepare a constitution for the United Government of Coridan; to submit the constitution to the people of Coridan for adoption or rejection; to prepare for the admission of Coridan as a member of the Federation; to make an appropriation; and setting an effective date, approved and adopted by a vote of the people of Coridan in the election held on Stardate 3411.3" is hereby found to be in conformity with the Articles of Federation, and is hereby accepted, ratified, and confirmed.

"We had police officers on Tarsus IV," Reilly said, "but before the crisis they were more like guards you'd find in an ancient shopping mall. They didn't even carry guns." In the wake of the populace's panic, Kodos turned the local security forces into a militia. He issued them weapons and commanded them to maintain order. He then called the ruling council together and told them that he had determined that their food supply would last long enough for help to arrive only if their population was halved.

Seth Rivel, a scientist who survived the crisis and made his report to the Federation, relayed this meeting. "I was stunned," Rivel said. "I looked around at the other members of the council, trying to see if I was the only one hearing that he was really suggesting killing half of the population.

"I barely knew Kodos," Rivel said. "He had seemed very cold to me, but not this cold." Before the council could do anything, Kodos declared martial law. He did not need the ruling council's consent, and had already made his own list of who would live and who would die.

The late biologist Thomas Leighton, also a survivor of Tarsus IV, made a contribution to the living witness project before his death: "I was thirteen; I was goofing around with a friend, and even though we knew something bad was going on, we were too young to really comprehend it."

Without revealing why, Kodos ordered 4,000 colonists to report to the main square of the colony. "My parents were called, but I wasn't," Leighton said, "so I was naturally curious what was going on. When you're a kid, you don't like to be left out." Leighton and his friend James Kirk, also thirteen, who was living on the planet with his mother, hid near the town square to spy on the crowd.

Kodos appeared before the colonists and told the 4,000 that their lives would be sacrificed so that the "more valuable" members of the colony could live. Then the militia was ordered to kill them. "They turned their energy weapons on the crowd," Leighton said, "and I screamed. My parents had been burned alive." Startled at the boy's scream, a militia member turned and fired at Leighton. Kirk tackled his friend to the ground—the beam from the weapon only searing his face instead of killing him.

Those colonists Kodos spared were horrified. Their lives had been bought at a terrible cost. But they were also afraid, and did nothing to rebel against the new order.

Kodos, meanwhile, was organizing the strict rationing of the available food when he received a communication from Starfleet.

"Spoke to Governor Kodos today," Captain Robert April recorded in his log, "and informed him that the *Enterprise* was already on its way. He seemed surprised at how fast we were going to get there. I guess news of the *Constitution* class hasn't made it out this far."

There is no clear record of the following events, but when Robert April beamed down to Tarsus IV all that was left of "Kodos the Executioner" was a body burned beyond recognition.*

***AUTHOR'S NOTE:** It was later discovered that Kodos had successfully faked his own death. He survived as a Shakespearean actor who traveled with a small theater company. Thomas Leighton and James Kirk would be the men responsible for discovering his true identity. But before he could be brought to justice, he was accidentally killed.

Leighton, carrying the physical and emotional scars of the traumatic experience, became a researcher dedicated to ending the threat of famine in the Galaxy. His friend James Kirk would take a different path.

FORBIDDEN PLANET

April finished his first five-year mission, but during the course of it he fell in love and married his ship's chief medical officer, Sarah Poole. When Starfleet Command offered him promotion to admiral—a position that would keep him on Earth—April took it, with the expressed desire to start a family. His replacement on the *U.S.S. Enterprise* was his first officer, Christopher Pike.

In one of his assignments, Pike would become acquainted with one of the most unusual—and dangerous—species in the Galaxy.*

The *S.S. Columbia* was a survey vessel commissioned for scientific study by the American Continent Institute in the year 2230. In 2236, it was lost, not unlike so many ships that ventured out beyond the rim of the Federation during that period.

In 2254, under the command of Captain Pike, the *U.S.S. Enterprise* received what they thought was a distress call from this forgotten ship. "We followed the distress call to the planet Talos IV," Pike stated in his logs, "where we quickly discovered that it was a trap set by the Talosians to capture me."

In captivity, Captain Pike learned a terrible secret about the Talosians—their intelligence had developed to such a level that they were telepathic, and could project illusions into the minds of others. The illusions were indistinguishable from reality. "This society had lost the will to live," Pike said.

ABOVE: Captain Pike and two of his senior officers. ***AUTHOR'S NOTE:** Captain Pike's logs of the events that follow have only recently been declassified by Starfleet Command.

GENERAL ORDER 6

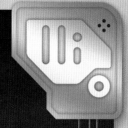

In the manufacture and maintenance of Starfleet ships and facilities, it is forbidden for Starfleet personnel to use resources supplied by a third party whose mining, manufacturing, and processing standards have not been judged to meet the minimum standards of safety and quality assurance set by Starfleet Command.

GENERAL ORDER 7

I: SPECIFICATIONS

The fourth planet of the Talos Star Group shall be considered off limits to Starfleet and Federation personnel. No vessel, under any condition, either emergency or otherwise, shall visit Talos IV.

a) Violations of this order also include but are not limited to:

1) Any attempt to make contact with denizens of Talos IV.
2) Any attempt to assist others in the violations listed herein.

II: PENALTY

The penalty of any and all infractions of General Order 7 is death. Procedural details to be determined by the current Starfleet Commander-in-Chief.

"They projected illusions into my mind, and then vicariously experienced my emotional response to the illusions they were projecting."

Pike and his crew were eventually released because the Talosians found Humans unsuitable to be kept as captives. When Pike's report made it back to Starfleet Command, Admiral April flagged it for the Federation Council. The Talosians' abilities were truly remarkable, and—it was determined—very dangerous. Though Starfleet was devoted to advancement, this was something that no one in the Federation was ready for. Based on the recommendation of both Captain Pike and Admiral April, travel to Talos IV was to be severely restricted.

The individual members of the Federation Council were not disposed to accept this recommendation. The Tellarites saw the potential for profit in such mind abilities, as did the Andorians and some of the smaller worlds. But the Federation President, Kristof Blaque, knew that if the power of the Talosians was as potentially destructive as his experts said, he needed to ensure it never spread beyond that world.

President Blaque made a motion that the Federation Council establish heavy security regarding information about Talos IV, and the death penalty for any Federation member that went there. The extreme nature of this motion was met with incredulity; those species who wanted access to Talos assumed there was no way it would pass. The death penalty had never been a part of the Federation judicial system. But Blaque was an experienced politician, and he lined up the necessary votes from the smaller worlds of the Federation, as well as Vulcan and Proxima. The motion passed by one vote. To this day, visiting Talos IV is the only death penalty offense in Federation law, and has made Talos IV known as the forbidden planet.

The same year that Talos IV became a forbidden planet, James Kirk would graduate from Starfleet Academy. This one officer—already a witness to history—would end up changing it himself.

JAMES T. KIRK

"I faced many challenges throughout my career," James Kirk told his official Starfleet biographer, "but the ones I experienced earliest in my life were the most profound." Though both of James Kirk's parents were Starfleet officers (Kirk himself was born on the *Einstein*-class ship, *U.S.S. Kelvin*), he had not considered a career in Starfleet until his experience on Tarsus IV.

OPPOSITE: An anomaly in an unusually open society, Starfleet Command made no effort to explain General Order 7 to its personnel for several decades. The fact that it carried the only death penalty for Starfleet officers only made it that much more tantalizing a mystery for cadets up through commodores. (Finding out the backstory behind this most perilous of Starfleet regulations was considered one of the perks of achieving the rank of admiral.) A reconsideration by the Federation Council in 2301 determined that the reasons behind General Order 7 should be revealed as an educational tool. However, the order is still in effect and violating it still carries the same penalty. It is interesting to note that the seemingly mundane General Order 6 has actually played a much more important role; it was put into effect after the reactor on the *U.S.S. Archon* exploded because it had used dilithium acquired by barter with an Orion trader.

"I was living on Tarsus IV with my mother, who was working there temporarily," Kirk said. "We'd just been through this horrible ordeal. Though we'd both been chosen to survive, many of our friends had died."

He was standing with his mother when the landing party from the *Enterprise* beamed into the town square. "I could feel her relief," Kirk said. "And I knew when we saw the captain that everything was going to be all right." It was this moment, he said, that made him want to join Starfleet.

The Tarsus IV experience was the key event in shaping the man who would come to exemplify Starfleet. Another formative event in Kirk's life would occur while he was a cadet at Starfleet Academy. It was Kirk's first exposure to the Klingon Empire, and it would serve both sides of the captain he would become: the warrior who continually challenged his Klingon adversaries, and the peacemaker, who nevertheless made extraordinary efforts to understand them.

The planet Axanar was at the far end of the Federation border with Klingon space. Unknown to the Federation, it was a subject world of the Klingon Empire. When the *U.S.S. Constitution*, under the command of Captain Garth of Izar, visited the system, two Klingon D5 ships and one Klingon D7 ship attacked. Garth, though outnumbered, defeated the Klingon ships. The Federation, fearing this stumble into a Klingon-controlled area would start another war, made a move to open talks with the Klingons. Normally, this would have been met with open contempt. But there was a new trend in Klingon politics.

The leader of the Klingon people during this period was a chancellor named Orak. As a very young man, Orak had been a prosecutor in the Klingon justice system. "He was an unusual Klingon in that he was very practiced in the art of politics, diversion, and deception," wrote Aleek Om, the Aurelian historian in his exhaustive treatise *Changing Spots: Klingons in the 23rd Century*. As Orak found his way onto the High Council, eventually moving to its leadership, he saw the wisdom in treading more carefully.

"Orak sought Klingons who viewed politics the way he did, as a game of deceit and deception," Aleek Om wrote. "As a result, the Klingon government became much more conniving during the period of Orak's rule." To Orak, the Federation had proven itself to be a very worthy adversary, and Orak ordered new tactics in dealing with them.

"He commissioned the training of spies who would be surgically altered to appear as Federation members," Om wrote. "Their job would be to both gather information and disrupt Federation initiatives." Meanwhile, Orak would talk "peace." The incident on Axanar gave him the opportunity he was looking for to divert the Federation's attention from his true motives.

So when the Klingons agreed to a peace conference regarding Axanar, it was a cause for great optimism in the Federation Council. This was the opportunity to build a bridge between the two governments. The Council went even further; information on and one-on-one experience with the Klingons was so rare, the Council directed Starfleet Commander April to send a group of Starfleet cadets along with the diplomats and other Starfleet officers. It was an opportunity to increase their understanding of a major adversary. James Kirk was one of these cadets.

"When I arrived at Axanar," Kirk said to his biographer, "it did a lot to cement my negative opinion of the Klingons."

The planet was a vast slave labor camp, its people growing food and mining resources for use by the Empire.

"I spoke to a few Axanars," Kirk said, "heard stories of the brutal treatment by the Klingons, the killing of hundreds of hostages for the tiniest act of rebellion, and the complete subversion of the Axanar culture beneath the heel of Klingon oppression." But he also saw that the Axanars were only producing basic resources for the Klingons.

"They weren't building spaceships," Kirk said, "they were growing a lot of food. It was clear that the Klingons had basic needs in their Empire. That maybe open trade was the solution to our problems with them." This observation, made in his report, moved up the chain of command and caught the attention of many in high places. And regardless of Orak's true intentions, at the time, the peace mission was considered a success, opening a dialogue with the Klingons that would continue for fifteen years.

Upon graduating from the Academy, Kirk served with Captain Stephen Garrovick, first on the *U.S.S. Republic*, and then on the *U.S.S. Farragut*. Garrovick is credited with instilling in Kirk both a reverence for intelligent life, as well as empathy for the needs of his own crew. But there was one final event as a lieutenant on the *Farragut* that changed Kirk and pushed him to become a great leader.

The *Farragut* was in orbit around the fourth planet in the Tycho star system when it was attacked by a gaseous creature. Kirk was on duty at phaser control when the creature attacked, killing over half of the *Farragut*'s crew, including Captain Garrovick.

"I hesitated when the cloud first appeared," Lieutenant Kirk said in his log entry. "If I hadn't, the captain and the rest of the crew who were killed would still be alive."

LEFT: Statue of Orak outside the Klingon Ministry of Intelligence on Qo'noS. **FOLLOWING SPREAD:** After the Klingons allied with the Federation, a treasure trove of information became available regarding their internal politics, including the many spy operations Orak had implemented. Added to the many qualifications of a Klingon warrior was a new virtue: guile.

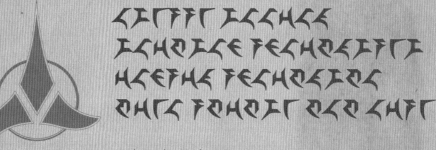

KLINGON SPY OPERATIONS

TRANSLATED FROM THE KLINGON

Klingon Secret Service Operations Report
Operative "Arne Darvin" (AKA Kron)

The High Command, due to the oppression of the Organian Peace Treaty, has been forced into a position in which we need to not only develop planets ourselves, but also undermine the Federation efforts to do the same. In accordance with this, the General of Intelligence Operations has initiated a plan to place a soldier under a Human alias in the agricultural administration of the Federation. This stroke of genius will allow one of our soldiers to infiltrate a Federation administrative division with limited security precautions but substantial influence on the efforts of the Earthers.

To determine the appropriate candidate for our substitution, we intercepted communication traffic from the Federation Diplomatic Corps (one of their "peace-loving" bureaucracies) accepting an application from a Human from Proxima Centauri named Arne Darvin. Photographic, biological, and biographic information was gathered by the Intelligence Service, and a physically appropriate soldier named Kron was chosen to undergo surgical transformation in order to become identical to Darvin.

When en route to Earth to begin his training in the Federation Diplomatic Corps, a cloaked bird-of-prey, the B'rel, secretly beamed the true Darvin off the ship and replaced him with Kron. The substitution was undetected, and Kron began his training in the Federation Diplomatic Corps. The true Darvin was immediately executed.

With a focus in agriculture, Kron as Darvin excelled in the undemanding training of the Earthers, and had his choice of assignments on graduation. This week, after five years in the field, Kron was given an appointment as an assistant to the Undersecretary for Agricultural Affairs, a weakling Human whom they let govern development in the Federation sector that borders the Empire. Kron will transmit necessary information to us as needed.

S.S. VALIANT/SHIP RECORDER

STARFLEET LOG NO 44307.28R13

Transcript of *S.S. Valiant* ship recorder
Stardate 1350.2
Transcription completed by Lieutenant Lloyd Alden, Communications Officer *U.S.S. Enterprise*.

Note: The incompleteness of this transcript was due to the fact that the tapes were severely damaged beyond our ability to recover the information stored on them.

Scientist: Some kind of magnetic space storm, and it's pulling us in . . .
Helmsman: Losing helm control, sir . . .
Captain: All hands, go to full alert . . .
...
Navigator: . . . we're outside the Galaxy . . .
Captain: That's impossible . . . maybe interference from the storm has affected our instruments . . .
Navigator: Interference has cleared . . . it's confirmed . . . historic moment.
Captain: We can celebrate when the engines are repaired . . . set a course back to the Galaxy . . .
...
Doctor: I've counted seven dead, sir. What was it?
Captain: Some kind of negative barrier surrounding the Galaxy.
Doctor: Wait, a barrier around the Galaxy? I don't get it . . .
Captain: When I figure it out, I'll tell you . . .
...
Doctor: Wendy wasn't dead, she was in some kind of coma-like stasis.
Captain: Can I talk to her?
Doctor: Sure . . . can't believe how fast she's recovering . . .
...
Captain: . . . be good to have you back in engineering . . .
Wendy: Don't worry, we'll make it home.
Captain: What?
Wendy: You just said, "I don't know how we'll make it home," but we will.
...
Doctor: She read your mind?
Captain: . . . Check the computer records for anything on extrasensory perception . . .
...
Helmsman: . . . it was like the ship was steering itself . . .
Captain: . . . and she's still in the dispensary . . .
Doctor: . . . laughing at something all morning . . .
Captain: Get me that information about extrasensory perception . . .
Doctor: . . . not a lot . . .
Captain: . . . got to be something! Give me whatever you have!
...
Captain: . . . just us and her . . .
Doctor: . . . I can feel her in my head . . .
Captain: Computer, destruct sequence, code 1a . . .

Feelings of guilt had a profound effect on the young officer.

"I'd been kind of bookish and shy before that incident," Kirk said, "and above all, cautious. I sought to consciously change that. I pushed myself to take risks, to be more aggressive. I couldn't let something like that happen again." This conscious change in his attitude had an immediate effect on his career prospects. He became a clear and quick decision-maker, much more of a leader than he'd ever been. It was these combinations of qualities that eventually led him, at age thirty-one, to be the youngest Starfleet officer given command of a starship.

When Christopher Pike was elevated to fleet captain, Kirk was at the top of the promotion list. He was placed in command of the *Enterprise*. History would record that having this officer on this ship in this sector of space would be the greatest accidental contribution to history Starfleet would ever make.

THE RAPTOR'S RETURN

During the century after their war with Earth, Romulus had undergone many changes. Soon after the war, Praetor Gileus was deposed and replaced by a succession of failed leaders. In the early part of the twenty-third century a new praetor, Varus III, took power. The defeat at Cheron was still a painful memory for the Romulans, and Varus—with the power of the Romulan fleet behind him—had ridden a wave of resentment to the leadership of the Senate. He promised to return Romulus to its former glory.

The documentation the Federation has on internal Romulan politics in this era is limited, but indicates Varus was not as cautious a leader as Gileus was. One source, Pardek, is currently a Romulan senator. He filled in some of the blanks of this particular period in Romulan history at the request of Spock, a former Starfleet officer (who served with Pike and Kirk aboard *Enterprise*), now serving as a Federation ambassador.

"It was generally agreed that Varus was drunk with his own power," wrote Pardek, in a correspondence with

OPPOSITE: One of Kirk's first missions as captain of the *Enterprise* was a scientific expedition outside of the Galaxy, which ended up solving the two-centuries-old mystery of the fate of the original *S.S. Valiant*. The ship had kept a running record of all the interactions and orders among the crew, but most of it was destroyed in the tragedy that took the ship. Scientists later theorized that the "magnetic space storm" that the captain mentions in his log may in fact have been an unstable wormhole, which would help explain how an Earth ship from this period was able to reach the Galaxy's edge. **FOLLOWING SPREAD:** Part of a cache of documents smuggled out of the Romulan Empire, the following is a transcript of a speech recorded during a special secret session of the Romulan Senate. The speech lays out Varus's conclusion of the first agreement with the Klingons, and his plans to remake the Alpha Quadrant. The relationship between the Klingons and the Romulans was far from tranquil, but it did lead to the Romulans sharing cloaking technology with the Klingons, in exchange for the Klingons sharing the designs of their D7 ship. It is uncertain if Varus's use of the term "Earth Federation" was a deliberate attempt to identify the Federation as an Earth-centered Empire, or whether he truly believed it.

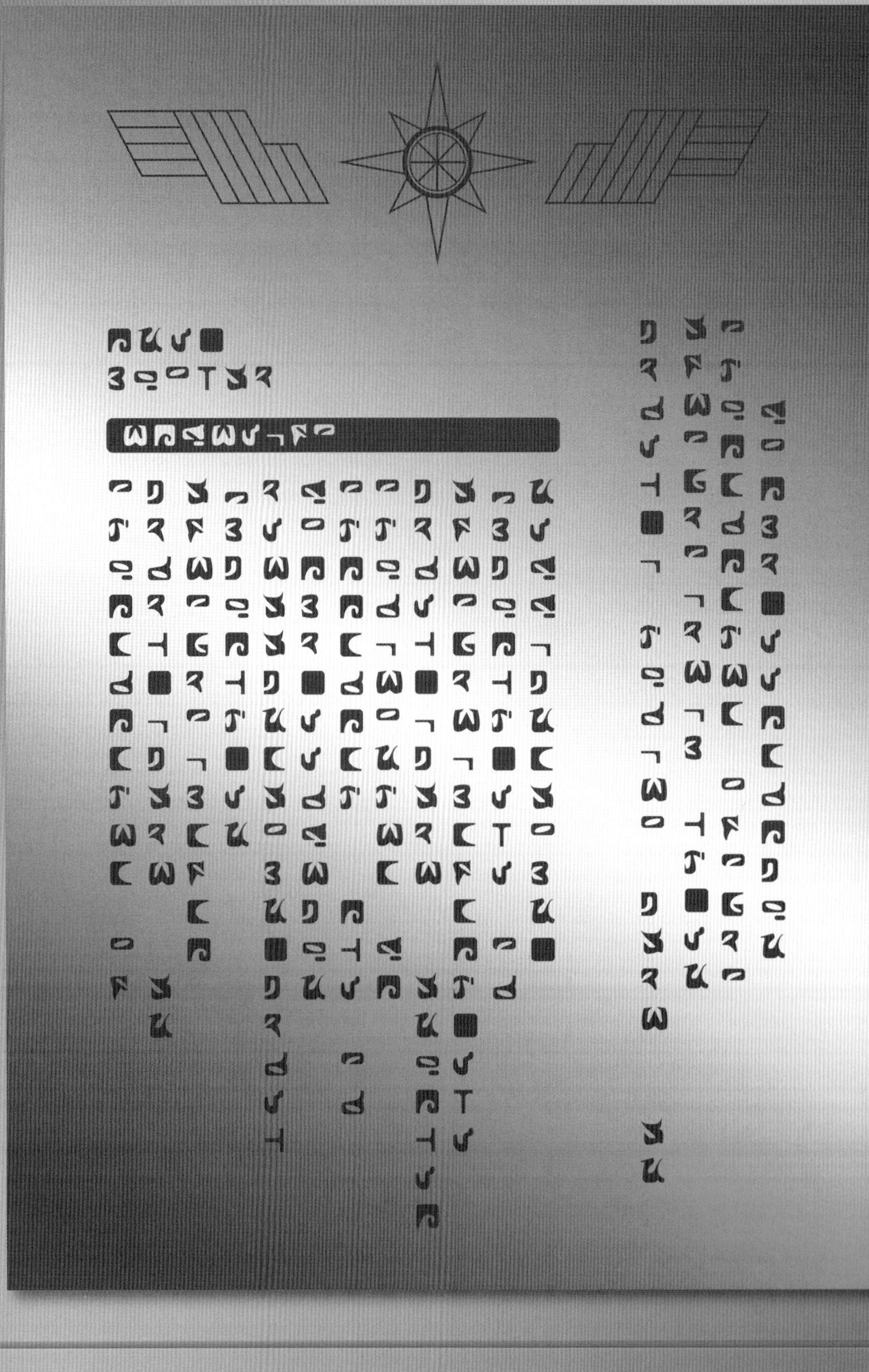

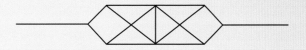

TRANSCRIPTION OF A SPEECH BY ROMULAN PRAETOR VARUS III

TRANSLATED FROM THE ROMULAN

My fellow Romulans,

I come to you to report on our victorious mission to the Klingon Empire. I have successfully concluded negotiations with the High Council, who pledge the Klingons will not interfere with any aggression we take against the Earth Federation.

<applause>

As part of this agreement, we have opened the door to trade with the Klingons, who will provide us with many tools that will be of use in the coming conflict.

<applause>

And the conflict is coming, I assure you. Our intelligence shows that the Earth Federation has begun a massive arms buildup. They have completed construction of twelve new battle cruisers whose sole mission is to exploit the worlds not already in the human grasp. Our origin world, Vulcan, is already completely subjugated, and it should be one of our primary goals to release our Vulcan brothers from the grip of the Human hand.

<applause>

The Humans are not satisfied with their defeat of the Romulan fleet at Cheron. They know it was pure luck that led them to victory, and that if they don't act soon, the Raptor will take its revenge. They will move against us, of that I am certain. So the thought has burned in my mind. Do we wait for this inevitable attack? Or do we take action? It is after careful consideration and consultation with the brilliant soldiers that I have chosen the latter path.

<sustained applause and cheering>

Our new flagship will destroy the Earth outposts along the Neutral Zone. The Earthmen will send one of their new battle cruisers, and our flagship will destroy it. While the Earthmen cry when their proudest technological achievement is turned to dust by Romulan ingenuity, we will return with an invasion force and take their world. With the Earthmen gone, and the illusion of their invincibility lifted from the eyes of their allies, they will fall to our Empire.

<sustained applause and cheering>

Spock. "Those members of the Senate who disagreed with him thought he was blindly going down the path of his forefathers, refusing to learn from their mistakes." He built ships and found planets to subjugate, all the while planning for another large-scale war.

"Unfortunately," Pardek wrote, "his own motivations dovetailed well with those of the senior military advisers, who were anxious for revenge against the Earth." Pardek told Spock that Romulus's division from the rest of the Galaxy had limited their information.

"The Romulan government and its people thought the Federation was really just another name for the Human Empire," wrote Pardek. "Varus, like his predecessor Gileus, thought gaining control of Earth's resources would solidify his power indefinitely."

Varus also had two new advantages: a new cloaking device and a deadly plasma weapon. Over the last century, a more advanced cloaking device had been developed with the help of new generations of Cheron shipbuilders. It would allow ships to cross into Federation space without being detected. The plasma weapon had already been proven completely effective at destroying ships and bases. A Romulan ship with both these attributes was the ultimate weapon.

"Varus was convinced by our military that this ship was indestructible," Pardek wrote, "that its attack would have to succeed." He was seduced into thinking no Federation ship could stand up to these weapons, and that the first attack would "send the Earthmen running scared," easy pickings for the Romulan fleet.

The Romulan flagship, named the *Algeron* in memory of Romulus's historic victory there, destroyed four of the outposts along the Neutral Zone. The *Enterprise*, under Kirk, was sent after it. Kirk was cautious; his orders stated that he was not allowed to enter the Neutral Zone. He was able to both obey this order and find the weaknesses in the supposedly indestructible ship. The ship was defeated, and the Romulan captain, in keeping with tradition, destroyed his own ship, and his crew with it. Kirk almost single-handedly had prevented a war.*

THE TWO-DAY WAR

During the same period that the Federation was fending off new threats from Romulus, the Klingon Empire was once again undergoing an internal change. Chancellor Orak had passed away, and after a battle for succession to the chancellorship, Koval—a member of a more traditional Klingon family—had seized power by killing the other challenger, a member of the Klaa family.

"The new chancellor had no patience for the long game that Orak had played," Aleek Om wrote, "and certainly had no patience for peace talks with the Federation." In 2267, as Klingon negotiators who had been appointed by Orak were ready for a compromise agreement to withdraw Klingon forces from the Disputed Area, Koval took control and changed course.

"In Koval's view, Klingons should take what they wanted," Aleek Om wrote, "and they wanted these systems. Koval was tired of the Federation restricting the Empire's trade opportunities. He believed the Federation was forcing the Klingons to negotiate." He ordered his ships to move across the border and attack.

Commander Kor, the chief military adviser to Koval,

was insistent that Klingon needed a base of operations. The only Class-M planet in the area was Organia—which they perceived as home to a weak humanoid race. Koval sent Kor with a fleet of eight ships to occupy it. At the same time, the Federation, alarmed by the Klingons' apparent intentions, ordered *Enterprise* to Organia in the vain hope that Captain Kirk could keep it out of Klingon control.

"In war with the Klingons, we were at a disadvantage," Kirk said. "We weren't going to set up a base without the Organians' permission. The Klingons, on the other hand, wouldn't ask."

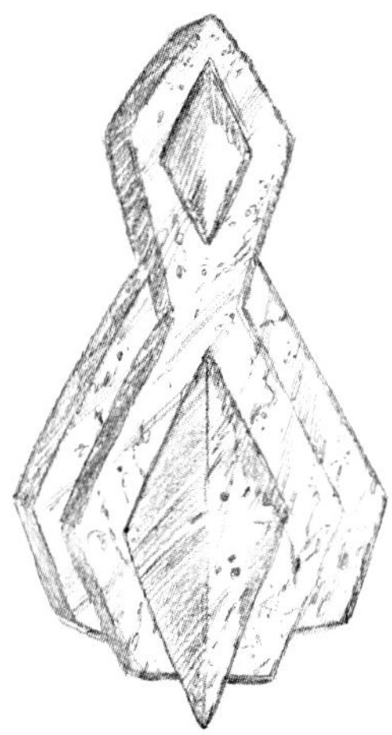

On Earth, the Federation Council, led by Bormenus of Andoria, had seen the negotiations with the Klingons breaking down and was ready to declare war after the first attack. "As a boy I had heard about the Human minister Nathan Samuels and how he reacted to the attack on Starbase 1," Bormenus said in an interview with the Federation News Service. "An Andorian would never make that mistake."

As fleets of ships moved to fight over Organia, what the two sides could not know was that the Organians were not a weak, primitive people. They were, in fact, so highly advanced that they had evolved beyond the need of physical bodies. They only took on their primitive humanoid forms to put visitors at ease. As the two fleets moved toward each other to engage in battle in the space above their planet, the Organians intervened.

On Earth, in the president's office in Paris, Bormenus was monitoring the reports from the front when he received a message from his fleet that it had been immobilized.

"We were trying to figure out what in hell was going on," Bormenus said in an interview, "when this elderly humanoid appeared in front of us." He said his name was Ayelborne and that he was an Organian. "I reached for a knife to defend myself, and it was like fire. The Organian asked me to listen to him, and, left with no choice, I did."

At the same time, in the High Council Chamber on Qo'noS, Koval was receiving the same report about his own ships—as well as the same visitor. "Koval made a very aggressive move against Ayelborne," Aleek Om wrote, "running to grab his *bat'leth* sword, but it was too hot to hold. Ayelborne asked him to listen. Koval then tried to tackle Ayelborne, who was too hot to touch." Finally, holding his hands in pain, Koval listened.

Ayelborne simultaneously ordered the leaders to communicate with each other and cease hostilities or he would

ABOVE: Symbol of the House of Koval, later adopted by his descendant Mogh.* **AUTHOR'S NOTE:** This engagement would reveal the secret that had been kept for a century: that the Romulans and the Vulcans were the same species. It would have a profound effect on Kirk's half-Vulcan first officer, the future Ambassador Spock, who would seek more information about his Romulan brethren and lead him to form a relationship with Pardek, whom Spock would meet during the Khitomer Peace summit.

immobilize all their ships and stations. Everywhere. To prove it, he shut down power in all of Paris and in the Klingon capital city.

"The lights went out for five minutes. We had no power anywhere," Bormenus said, "and when they came back on, Ayelborne was gone, and I was staring at a Klingon on my viewscreen." Bormenus and Koval also both held a unique disk made of an unknown material, on which floated the words "Organian Peace Treaty between the United Federation of Planets and the Klingon Empire." When the men touched the surface of the disk, subsequent clauses of the treaty appeared, each in their own language, and Ayelborne's voice read them out loud. Bormenus and Koval studied it and each other for a moment, then Bormenus said, "We should probably figure out how to sign this."

The whole affair was an embarrassment to both sides.

"I grew up in a Federation that expounded peace as a way of life," Kirk said to his biographer just before his death, "and here I was, ready, almost anxious to go to war. I knew I had a lot of animosity toward the Klingons, and unfortunately it was only going to get worse."

On its surface, the Organian Peace Treaty outlined terms for the Klingons and the Federation to co-exist peacefully.

ABOVE: Starfleet and Klingon ships face off in orbit above Organia. **OPPOSITE:** Unlike any other document of its kind in history, the Organian Peace Treaty was not mutually negotiated by two parties, nor was it a treaty where a victor would impose his will on the defeated. It was an imposed peace by a third party on two warring parties. It was also recorded on a very advanced disk whose technology remains a mystery to this day, as it is able to read the mind of whoever is viewing it and present the treaty in the viewer's native language. This excerpt illustrates one of many provisions that were intended to inspire the necessary fear to keep Klingons and the Federation from again becoming openly aggressive in their actions against the other. The phrase "permanently returned to their homeworld" was just vague and threatening enough to be a cause of great concern to both parties.

WORLDS IN DISPUTE

ALL WORLDS CURRENTLY IN THE PREVIOUSLY DESCRIBED DISPUTED AREA BETWEEN THE TWO PARTIES ARE NOW CONSIDERED NEUTRAL.

FURTHER, ANY WORLDS THAT MAY BE DISCOVERED FROM THIS POINT FORWARD THAT LIE IN THE ONE PARSEC OVERLAP BETWEEN THE NEAREST FEDERATION AND KLINGON OUTPOSTS SHALL BE CONSIDERED NEUTRAL.

NO PARTY MAY SEEK TO USE A NEW WORLD FOR MILITARY PURPOSES.

IF BOTH PARTIES SEEK TO MAKE USE OF THE WORLD TO PROVIDE SUSTENANCE TO THEIR CIVILIZATION,

THEY MUST MAKE A CASE TO THE ORGANIAN COUNCIL OF ELDERS THAT THEIR PLANS FOR IT ARE EFFICIENT AND NON-MILITARISTIC.

ANY ATTEMPT TO VIOLATE THIS SECTION OF THE AGREEMENT WILL RESULT IN THE PERMANENT IMMOBILIZATION OF THE OFFENDING PARTY'S FLEETS AND SPACE HABITATS.

ALL BEINGS BELONGING TO THE OFFENDING PARTY'S SPECIES WILL BE IMMEDIATELY AND PERMANENTLY RETURNED TO THEIR HOMEWORLD.

If a government wanted to lay claim to a planet, it would have to prove it could develop it most efficiently. It also forced each government to allow the other species access to their facilities.

The Klingons immediately took advantage of the treaty. "It was then that Koval was thankful to the vast spy network that Orak had set up," Aleek Om wrote, "and he set out to move in on planets that weren't even in the Klingon sphere of influence, but which the Federation had no claim to." The Klingons made inroads to many of them, such as the planets Capella and Neural.

"We were all very frustrated by the Klingons attempts to circumnavigate the treaty," Kirk said. "Their freedom of movement in Federation space unsettled a lot of people. It was not a good time." It also didn't seem that the Organians were interested in enforcing the treaty.

"They put this thing around our necks," Bormenus said, "and since we respect the law, we followed it. Meanwhile, the Klingons were making us look like fools and scaring our population with their intrusions. Something had to be done."

Around this time, the planet Coridan was seeking admission to the Federation, and Bormenus saw an opportunity. "I knew that the basis for much of the conflict between the Federation and the Klingon Empire were the planets in the Disputed Area that had large sources of dilithium." Coridan, it turned out, had an abundance of dilithium, and it was nowhere near the Klingons'.

"If I could get the Federation another source of dilithium, I could give up the Disputed Area, giving something to the Klingons in exchange for a new treaty that would keep them in their borders." Bormenus led Coridan through the admissions process, and it became a Federation member.

Bormenus and the Federation Council then made its proposal to the Klingons. The Federation would give up several worlds in the Disputed Area. In exchange, the Klingons would agree to a Neutral Zone like the one between Romulus

OPPOSITE: The planet Capella IV was of interest to both the Klingons and the Federation because it had a rich source of the rare element topaline, which many civilizations needed for their life-support systems. As a result, the Klingons made a strong, though ultimately unsuccessful, play to acquire mining rights out from under the Federation. This competition mattered little to the Capellans, a rigid and primitive society whose awareness of intergalactic civilizations in no way affected their development (the planet was first visited by the *U.S.S. Archon*, before the establishment of the Prime Directive). In this excerpt from a mining agreement between Capella and the Federation, with almost anything in the Galaxy to choose from, the Capellans chose to trade for better metal to make swords. **FOLLOWING SPREAD:** One of the last incursions into Federation space by the Klingons before the establishment of the Neutral Zone involved the mission to annihilate the tribbles. Tribbles were a unique species, essentially balls of fur whose entire systems were devoted to reproduction. A tribble outside of its predatory environment with access to a food supply could reproduce a thousand-fold in a matter of days. Considered an annoyance by the Federation, the tribbles were deemed by the Klingons a plague to be wiped out. The "interloper" in the following report refers to a human trader named Cyrano Jones, who is the man responsible for first removing the tribbles from their home planet. It is of continued debate whether the Federation was aware of this Klingon mission and did nothing to stop it.

HEREIN

THE UNITED FEDERATION OF PLANETS

AND

THE TEN TRIBES OF CAPELLA

I) On this day, the seventh day in the Age of his reign, that the High Teer shall allow the United Federation of Planets to establish a MINING COLONY on Capella IV, the purpose of which is to extract the element TOPALINE.

A) Only that element shall be mined, unless other elements are discovered during the term of this agreement and later determined by both parties to fall within the limits of this agreement.

B) Location and physical limitations of colony have been mutually agreed upon as described in Appendix A.

II) In exchange for the rights to establish said colony, the United Federation of Planets does agree to provide the following:

A) 1 metric ton Castrodinium per annum.

B) 1 metric ton Trititanium per annum.

C) Federation will provide technical instructions in the use of the above materials to manufacture handheld weapons (including but not limited to knives, swords, kligat). Such manufacturing, as described in Appendix B, will not significantly exceed the technological limitations of the Capellan people.

III) This agreement shall stay in effect for the duration of the rule of the High Teer and his successors, and shall only be amended through the process as described in Appendix C.

Agreed and signed,

James T. Kirk
United Federation of Planets Representative

Eleen Akaar
Regent
Representing the High Teer Leonard James Akaar

THE DESTRUCTION OF THE TRIBBLE HOME PLANET

TRANSLATED FROM THE KLINGON

Report to the High Command

I, Koloth, captain of the *IKS G'roth*, have completed the mission set forth by the High Command. The plague has ended!

I took my fleet of five D7 warships and we began our hunt where the plague began, on the Federation Station designated K-7. There, we found the interloper. He was pathetically trying to undo the plague that had consumed this station, by ferrying them back to the plague's home planet. We finished his job for him, and destroyed every tribble on that station. The pitiful humans stood by helplessly as my loyal Klingon soldiers vaporized them all, as the tribbles' screams were suddenly silenced.

We extracted the name of every world where the interloper had brought the plague and set out to find and destroy them. For eight months we scoured worlds for signs of the plague, and only until we were certain that we'd eradicated every one did we move on.

Finally, we ended our campaign at the hell that spawned this vile menace. I myself beamed down to the surface to view this terrible place, and stood on a mountaintop as our D7 ships entered the atmosphere and laid waste to the land with their disrupter fire. It was a glorious sight. The once-green land was a burnt black where nothing survived. Our scientists remarked that there were over a billion species of flora and fauna on this world before we attacked, and all that remained after we were through was blackened cinders. It was glorious! The plague has ended!

MEMORY ALPHA LCARS HARD COPY EXTRACT

ORIGINAL SOURCE: FEDERATION NEWS SERVICE	4597.1

GALACTIC PEACEMAKER

Ambassador Robert Fox says big problems don't always require big solutions

By Michael Metlay

"Diplomacy," Robert Fox, Federation ambassador-at-large, is fond of saying, "is best left to the diplomats." We're in a shuttlecraft on our way through the atmosphere of Fox's testament of the truth of this statement: Nimbus III.

The first planet to be jointly developed by the Federation, the Klingon Empire, and the Romulan Star Empire, Nimbus III was the brainchild of Fox, a thirty-year veteran of galactic politics. When the Neutral Zone was established with the Klingon Empire, Nimbus III was the one planet that fell within the common area of the Neutral Zones between the Klingons, the Romulans, and the Federation. When Fox heard of this planet's existence, he had an idea. Since none of the governments had claimed the planet, perhaps they should all claim it. With the Federation Council's permission, he personally contacted the Klingons and the Romulans. Miraculously, they all agreed. What drove Fox to pursue this grand project?

"I've watched people die in unnecessary conflicts involving these three great powers. These conflicts could've been settled if there'd been an avenue for negotiations." Fox says Nimbus III will be "the permanent table where a Klingon, a Federation member, and a Romulan will always be able to meet, to share a drink, and to solve their differences."

Our shuttle lands outside the town square of a city that Fox himself has named Paradise. The planet itself seems far from that description; it is hot and desolate, with only sand dunes visible around the site of the future city. This does not worry Fox. "We've terraformed worlds before, and we'll do it again. I named the city 'Paradise' because that's what this planet's going to look like in a few years."

Each government will be represented by one delegate, and Fox is putting his reputation on the line by taking the role of the Federation's first ambassador to Nimbus III. Asked why he is so confident that this project will lead to a lasting peace between three governments who have never gotten along, Fox tells a story from his own career.

"Recently, I single-handedly ended a war between Eminiar and Vendikar," Fox says. "They'd been at war for five centuries. We've only known the Klingons and the Romulans for one." Fox smiles. "This is a piece of cake."

and the Federation. Klingons would no longer be allowed in Federation space or be free to influence events on the worlds of the Federation. The Klingons, meanwhile, would receive a large supply of dilithium, compensating them for the source they were deprived of following the Organian Peace Treaty. The Klingon High Council readily agreed.

Once the treaty had been negotiated, Koval and Bormenus, along with a considerable entourage of security, went to Organia, looking to receive the blessing of the powerful beings. No Organian deigned to greet them. "After about an hour of standing around their primitive town square," Bormenus said, "Koval took the document from me, signed it, and said he was leaving."

THE PLANET OF GALACTIC PEACE

When the Neutral Zone with the Klingons was established, it was noted by many people that it appeared to be a geographic extension of the Romulan Neutral Zone. Where the three territories met was the Nimbus system, the third planet of which was an uninhabited Class-M world. Ambassador Robert Fox, diplomat-at-large for the Federation, saw an opportunity: this planet could be developed by all three in partnership. He hoped this would be the beginning of a new age, with the three governments learning to work together. The Federation gave Fox approval to try.

After much negotiation it was determined that a Romulan, Klingon, and Federation representative would serve as the ruling council. Settlers would be welcomed and encouraged to work together to build this new world. Fox himself would be the first Federation representative. He would end up regretting the entire thing.

One of the reasons that Nimbus III had never been exploited is that it is remarkably free of anything of value. The settlers who arrived there found nothing useful, and those that remained did so because they had nowhere else to go. Though it did little to further the cause of peace, the three governments dutifully continued to send representatives.

Although the Romulans would stay quiet a very long time, the Klingon-Federation peace was more volatile. "Most of us knew that Nimbus III was a joke," Kirk said. "My generation was smart enough not to trust the Klingons. They'd tried to fool us too many times." Kirk's attitude was prevalent among the Federation population, and over the next twenty years the embers of war between the Federation and the Klingons would continue to glow. At the moment where peace looked like it might finally come, members of both sides looked to fan the embers to flame.

OPPOSITE: Ambassador Robert Fox fought to establish Nimbus III as a representation of the new age of peace between Romulus, Qo'noS, and the Federation. Its establishment, however, was marred by a lack of planning, poor execution, and what some view as Fox's focus on his legacy rather than a true vision for the community. Its failure is a mark on the history of the Federation's peacemaking efforts. This article was written during the period that Fox—and many others—still had high hopes for its success. **FOLLOWING SPREAD:** The Orion Syndicate was as successful a form of capitalism as has existed in the Galaxy. Unfortunately, like many businesspeople before them, they tried to influence governments to guarantee their profits. The following opening page of the "business plan" laid out their intentions to stop the admission of Coridan to the Federation.

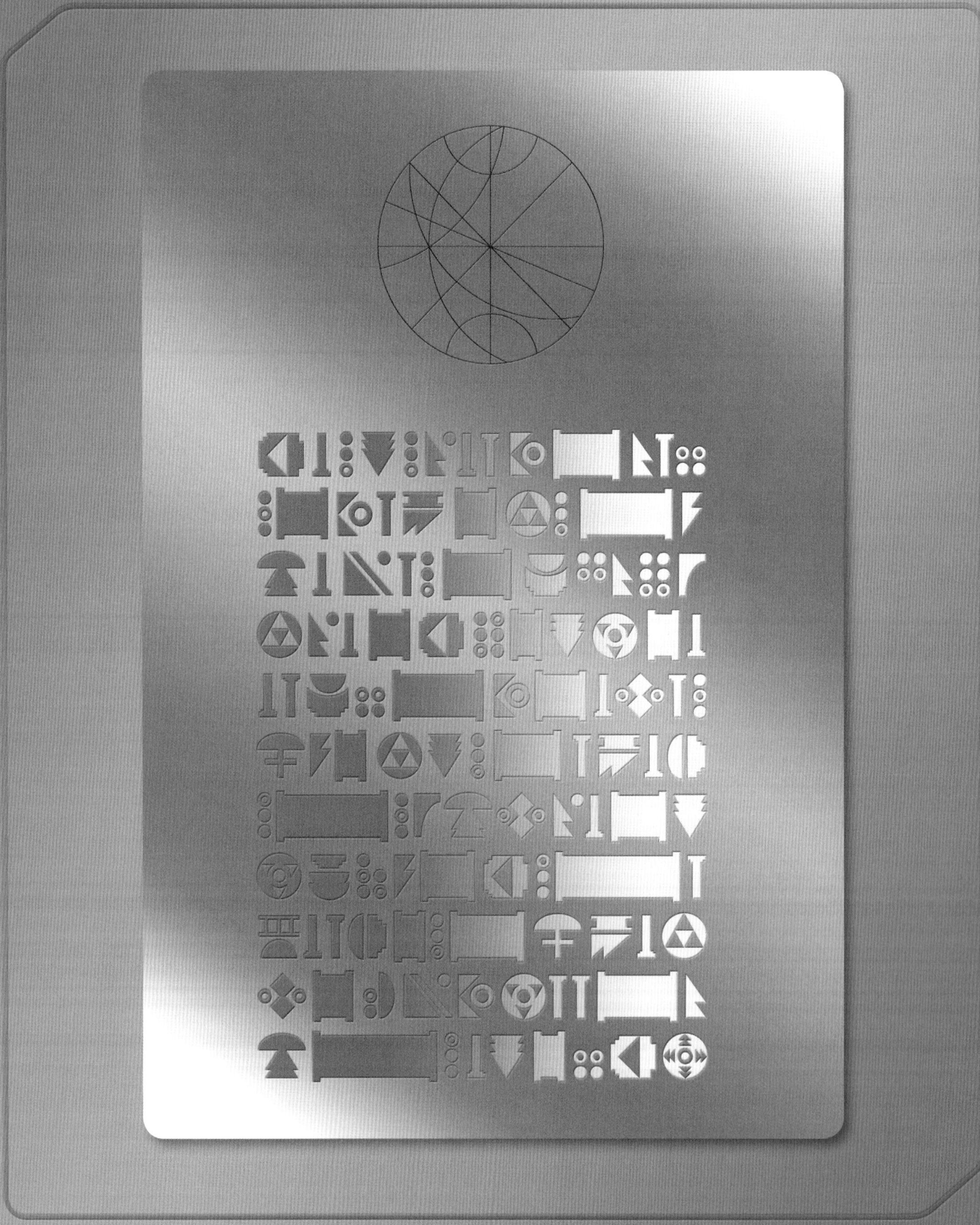

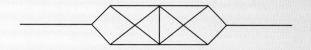

ORION SYNDICATE BUSINESS PLAN
ITNEY SHEN'S DILITHIUM MINING CORPORATION

TRANSLATED FROM THE CORIDAN

EXECUTIVE SUMMARY

Itney Shen is one of the many Orion slave owners who has mined and processed dilithium for the Orion Syndicate. The company she has established, Itney Shen LLC, currently has 48 percent of the dilithium market in the Syndicate, and uses her covert dilithium mining operation on the planet Coridan to provide 93 percent of her product. According to member rules, she has provided 30 percent of her profits in this endeavor to the Syndicate accounts.

Coridan has applied for membership in the United Federation of Planets. Because this will almost certainly interfere with Itney Shen's operation on the planet, the company deems it necessary to ensure that Coridan's admission is unsuccessful. The company proposes to the Orion Syndicate that there is an opportunity in preventing Coridan's admission that will profit the entire Syndicate.

OBJECTIVES

Prevent Coridan's admission to the Federation

Sow distrust among Federation members

Instigate an interplanetary war between two or more of the Federation members

Sell dilithium to any interested party during this conflict

MISSION

Itney Shen LLC seeks to send an operative disguised as a delegate to the conference where Coridan's admission to the Federation will be determined. En route to this conference, this operative will eliminate other delegates, ensuring their rivals are to blame. The operative will continue his disruption until success is assured both in undermining the admission and sowing the seeds of an interplanetary conflict.

In the event that the operative is unsuccessful or captured, Itney Shen will provide a ship to attack and destroy the vessel conveying the delegates to their conference. Though this is less likely to start a war, it will protect the Orions' neutrality.

CHAPTER V

THE NEW ERA

2290–2311

"Only Nixon could go to China."

—Ancient Vulcan proverb

OPPOSITE: An artist's rendition of Starfleet's greatest vessels.

By the end of the twenty-third century, the Federation and the Klingon Empire were on a road to eventual mutual destruction. The hostilities between the two had never been sufficiently resolved, so they stayed on either side of the Neutral Zone waiting for a sign from the other that war would be a necessity. With tensions this high, there was plenty of opportunity for misunderstanding.

THE GENESIS CRISIS

In the mid-2280s, a mother-and-son scientific team, Drs. Carol and David Marcus, made an incredible breakthrough in genetic engineering. In laboratory experiments they succeeded in reconfiguring inanimate matter on the subatomic level to create life-generating matter of equal mass.

"They can create worlds," Federation President Hiram Roth said in a closed session of the Federation Council. "This could solve so many problems regarding living space and food supply, we have to support it." The Federation Council approved the granting of facilities and resources to take their experiments to completion. The Marcuses developed and constructed the Genesis Device, which could theoretically transform a dead planet into a living one. The Federation starship *Reliant* was detailed to help them find a suitable planet to conduct their experiment. What *Reliant* found instead was a lost piece of history that would send the Galaxy to the precipice of war.

BELOW: The DY-100 ship christened *S.S. Botany Bay* by the genetic supermen who stole it in 1996.

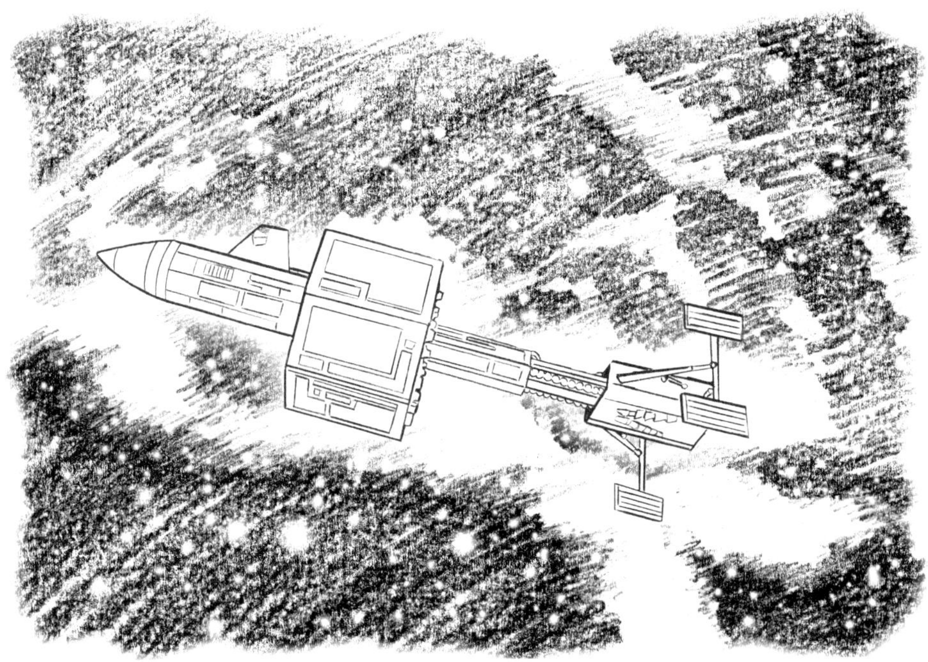

THE RETURN OF KHAN

In 2267, the *U.S.S. Enterprise* discovered a DY-100 ship from the twentieth century. On board were seventy-two genetic supermen and -women in suspended animation, including the dictator Khan Noonien Singh, who had escaped capture and prosecution following the Eugenics Wars by launching themselves into space.

Rather than imprisoning them, Captain Kirk gave them a second chance by marooning them on Ceti Alpha V, a remote, barren world, to build their own society. "Here were these incredibly intelligent, resourceful men and women," Kirk said to his biographer, "and it seemed like a huge waste to lock them up for the rest of their lives." Kirk would regret his decision.

Fifteen years later, *Reliant* inadvertently came upon Khan and his followers. The group seized the ship, killed the captain, and stole the Genesis Device. It was up to a now-Admiral Kirk to defeat him. "It was a monstrous error," Kirk said. "They were killers, murderers on a global scale, they didn't deserve my mercy and I paid—the *Reliant*'s crew paid—a terrible price for my hubris."

Though Khan was eventually killed, innocent lives were lost on both *Enterprise* and *Reliant*, and Kirk was unable to stop him from detonating the device. The process of the detonation transformed the planetary nebula Mutara into a Class-M world, which the Federation named the "Genesis Planet."

The ramifications of the Federation's ability to create a planet were felt throughout the quadrant, sparking a great controversy. If the Genesis Device were to be used on a planet where life already existed, the existing life would be wiped out. Khan's involvement with the Genesis Planet made a natural connection to the dangers of genetic engineering.

Concerned members of the Council had the same questions cautious Earthlings had had in the twentieth century: had the Federation moved too quickly into an area that was ethically dubious? "It was politically explosive," Hiram Roth said in an interview with this author. "Politicians had perverted the very noble goals of this project."

ABOVE: Khan Noonien Singh, as he appeared after fifteen years stranded on Ceti Alpha V.

The Andorian and Tellarite ambassadors to the Council, who had been reticent to approve funding the Genesis Project, felt their fears had been justified and lobbied hard to abandon the project. "It was a political quagmire," Roth said, "and the only way out was to walk away from it. It was a loss to the Federation."

But it was too late to entirely put the genie back in the bottle: the Klingons and the Romulans were both extremely concerned when they learned of the existence of the device. They assumed the Federation had developed it as a weapon—one that they would now always have in their arsenal. The Romulans took a restrained approach. For the first time, the Romulan government opened full diplomatic relations with the Federation, sending an ambassador to the Council, which the Federation welcomed. However, Romulan Ambassador Nanclus's job wasn't diplomacy; he was to use his position to run a spy network and gather as much information as he could on what the Federation plans were.

The Klingons were less circumspect. Their ambassador, Kamarag, in a session of the Federation Council, openly accused the Federation of planning an attack on the Klingon Homeworld.

"Kamarag was worried about the annihilation of his people," Hiram Roth said, "and frankly, I could understand why he wasn't buying our explanation that this was a science experiment. It didn't sound believable."

At home, the Klingons began gearing up for war, pulling ships from all corners of the Empire and bringing them to the Neutral Zone. Admiral Lance Cartwright, commander-in-chief of Starfleet Command, reconfigured Starfleet forces to counter the Klingon "wall of ships" with an even greater number of ships and stations in the hope that the Klingons would think twice about crossing into Federation territory.

As Hiram Roth's term came to an end, he saw his chances to bring a lasting peace fade. "War is not inevitable," he said in one of his final speeches to the Council. "We must commit ourselves to at least attempting a lasting peace."

BELOW: Federation President Hiram Roth and Trill Representative to the Federation Council Curzon Dax.

THE KORVAT TALKS

Roth had come up through the Federation diplomatic corps, and had served as ambassador to Trill in the 2260s, when it was a relatively new member of the Federation.

"The Trill have a uniquely peaceful culture," Roth said. "They keep to themselves about many things, but it does not ever seem to get in the way of a thriving diplomatic relationship."

When Roth became president, he naturally developed a close relationship with the Trill ambassador to the Federation Council, a young man named Curzon Dax. Though Curzon was only in his twenties, Roth often found himself seeking the young man's counsel, especially on the problems with the Klingons. "He seemed to me," Roth said, "to have wisdom beyond his years."

In 2289, the last year of his term as president, Roth approached the Klingon ambassador for one more chance at negotiations. Kamarag went to his government, which agreed to receive a Federation delegation on the Korvat colony. Despite his youth, Roth sent Dax to lead the talks. Representing the Klingon Empire were two of its generals, Kang and Koloth, and a junior member of the High Council, Gorkon. Though Gorkon would later play a large role in Klingon politics, in these peace talks Kang and Koloth took center stage.

According to Dax's report to the Council, Kang, Koloth, and Gorkon were initially aghast at the stripling sitting across from them. "I could see it in their faces that they saw a child," Dax wrote in a personal account of the meeting. "Interesting thing about Klingons: they won't accept someone if they're too young or too old." Dax dismissed their insults and suggested they get started.

"Kang began a long diatribe on the Federation's crimes against the Klingon Empire. I wasn't sure how long it was going to go on. He was only up to [the battle of] Donatu [V] when I decided I had enough." Curzon Dax got up from the table, turned his back on Kang, and left the room.

"I knew this would provoke a reaction," Dax wrote, "but I was frankly unprepared." Kang was furious. He leapt over the table and chased Dax out into the hallway. Kang tackled him to the floor, holding a blade to the young man's throat.

Witnesses to the event said Kang growled, "Is this how the Federation seeks to make a treaty?" Dax looked him in the eye and said, in colorful language, that the negotiations would begin once Kang was finished releasing gas from his mouth. Koloth, who had followed Kang into the hallway, broke out in laughter, and Kang did the same. They returned to the bargaining table, and it was the beginning of a long-lasting relationship between the three men, one that would eventually pay great dividends to the Federation.

But the talks would have no immediate effect on the current conflict. "I learned later that before the talks even began the Klingon High Council had decided that war was the only option they wanted to pursue," recounted Roth.

Hiram Roth would leave his position as president without achieving peace. In the wake of the Genesis Device revelation, the leader of the Klingon military, General Chang—a formidable, experienced, and devious officer—convinced the High Council to greatly expand ship and weapon production and let no mediation undermine this.

Chang's plan was for a decisive first strike against the Federation, meaning a sharp increase in military manufacturing. The plan put an even greater strain on a Klingon economy already buckling under a huge military budget. And as much of ship production was centered on Qo'noS, this also put a strain on Praxis—the Klingon moon that was the chief energy production facility.

PRAXIS

Centuries before, when the Klingons first went into space, Praxis had been considered a gift from the Klingon gods. It was the first world visited by Klingon warriors and was miraculously found to have a rich mineral supply. Within fifty years, Klingons had set up an energy production facility to make use of the moon's vast supplies of pergium, topaline, and uranium. It was projected then that these elements would permanently fulfill the needs of the residents of Qo'noS—and it did for generations.

In time, however, advances in technology required a greater strain on the energy production and rather than developing alternative sources of energy, the Klingons continued to mine Praxis unceasingly. Eventually, the moon became an unstable shell, which led to instability in its core—and, in 2293, its eventual destruction when one of the moon's quantum reactors overloaded.

"I was assistant communications officer on Praxis," a Klingon named Kenk reported to the High Council. "I had just come on shift when the explosion occurred."

Kenk was from a family long known in the galaxy—his great-granduncle was Klaang, whose dishonorable return home by Jonathan Archer had earned his and his family's banishment to the moon station. Like his forebears, Kenk had the mundane job of routing communication traffic between the moon and the receiving stations on Qo'noS.

"My work is very routine," Kenk said. "When the explosion occurred, I assumed we were under attack."

Surrounded by wreckage and flame, burned and bleeding, "I crawled to the communication console to send out a warning." He did not know his actions that day would counter those of his ancestor over a hundred years before. He was taking the first step toward a permanent peace in the Galaxy.

The explosion from Praxis created a massive subspace shockwave that hit the *U.S.S. Excelsior*, returning from patrol in Beta Quadrant. When the ship's captain reported back to Starfleet on the destruction of Praxis, Starfleet and the Federation quickly realized that this would have a long-term devastating effect on Klingon society, and they did their best to project the outcome of the disaster.

Despite the widespread nature of the Klingon Empire, it was still highly centralized around Qo'noS. Ships were built in its orbital facilities, the government operated on the planet, and most of the Klingon population lived there. Without their moon transmitting energy, and with the intense amounts of delta rays now seeping into their atmosphere, the Federation estimated that the Klingons had no more than 50 years of survival on their planet.

Meanwhile, on Qo'noS, there was a struggle for power following Praxis's destruction. Despite the fact that Klingons had been over-taxing Praxis for generations, members of the High Council, with the help of General Chang, placed the blame at the feet of the current Chancellor B'rak. A Council member, Gorkon, challenged his leadership in open council and as is Klingon tradition, they fought. B'rak was killed. However, despite his adherence to the traditional Klingon method for taking power, Gorkon had a reputation for thoughtfulness and introspection unusual in a Klingon. It was now his job to solve the problem that had allowed him to become chancellor.

In the wake of the moon's explosion and the power shift on Qo'noS, the question as to how to proceed was brought before a secret session of the Federation Council. Recently released records of the meeting indicate disagreement among the members. Many had been victim to the Klingons' aggression. But Hiram Roth's successor as president, Ra-ghoratreii, prevailed on them that this was an opportunity for peace.

Ra-ghoratreii was an Efrosian, whose people had once been under the rule of the Klingon Empire, and successfully rebelled. The Klingons were reeling, he told the Council, and in order to save themselves they might be willing to make a lasting peace. The establishment of Gorkon as leader of the High Council had further cemented Ra-ghoratreii's belief that this was the time to broker peace with the Klingons. And as an Efrosian, Ra-ghoratreii spoke from a unique position; if he was willing to forgive, then so should the rest of the Council. The Federation Council voted unanimously to initiate a new peace treaty with the Klingons.

Recordings of the Council proceedings indicate that although Ambassador Sarek of Vulcan agreed with the president, he also said they needed to proceed cautiously.

"My husband is an experienced diplomat," his wife, Amanda (a Human), wrote in *Love and Logic*, her memoirs of the period. "He knew that to go to the Klingons first would make the Federation appear too weak, yet the Klingons were too proud to come to the Federation." He had to find an unofficial way to reach out and begin a dialogue with the Klingons that allowed the Federation to retain the upper hand but not so humiliate the Klingons that they would rather die than negotiate.

"When he told me he had suggested our son," Amanda wrote, "I was very proud. And also very frightened."

SPOCK

Sarek and Amanda's son was Spock. For many years, Spock had served aboard the *Enterprise*, first as science officer to Captain Christopher Pike, then as first officer to Captain James Kirk, then briefly as *Enterprise*'s captain himself. During that long period of starship service, he played an important role in bringing many worlds into the Federation: Eminiar VII, Zeon and Ekos, Beta III, Melkotia, as well as making first contact with dozens of others. As a member of Starfleet, he had already led an unofficial career as an "ambassador without portfolio." Sarek knew his son's background, and surmised that if the Federation used him to start a dialogue with the Klingons, it would serve the purpose of an official making an unofficial gesture—it gave the Federation cover.

FOLLOWING SPREAD: This letter is in Sarek's handwriting, written on a Vulcan substance similar in feel to paper but made out of the silk of a Vulcan arachnid. The words reveal nothing, but the action of it being handwritten and hand-delivered in the twenty-third century was a secret message from father to son that this matter was of the utmost importance. The inclusion of the regards of Spock's Human mother speaks to the depth of feeling Sarek had for his wife, Amanda. Vulcans would never do something so illogical.

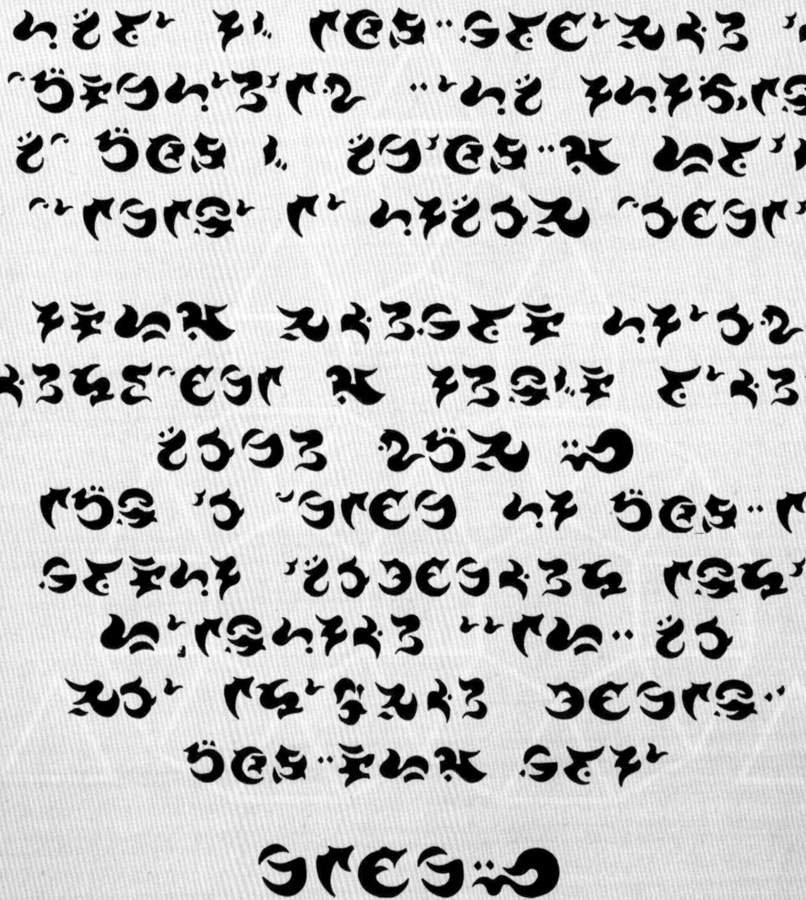

LETTER FROM SAREK TO SPOCK

TRANSLATED FROM THE VULCAN

Spock,

I request you travel to the Vulcan Embassy in San Francisco so that I may speak to you about current diplomatic affairs.

Your mother requested that I send you word of her love. I understand this seems illogical, as it is apparent you are already quite clear on her emotions concerning you, but she insisted.

Sarek

LEFT: James T. Kirk and his science officer Spock. **OPPOSITE:** A Klingon leader had never been given safe passage through Federation space, and Spock felt it necessary to give Gorkon some assurance besides his word that would guarantee his safety. Taking his lead from his father, Spock, using his intermediaries Curzon Dax and Kang, arranged to send Gorkon a handwritten invitation from the Federation president. Ra-ghoratreii wrote the letter in English because he didn't speak Klingon, and since his people, the Efrosians, had rebelled from Klingon oppression, writing in his native language might have been seen as an insult.

Sarek contacted Spock and educated him both on the plan and what he knew of the Klingon government. The new chancellor, Gorkon, was a warrior like all their leaders (he walked with the bone of a *krencha*, a large Klingon reptile that he himself had killed), but he had been the only High Council member at the negotiations at the Korvat colony. The fact that Gorkon had taken that risk in his past was their one glimmer of possibility.

"Sarek then told Spock that he would have to reach out to Gorkon on his own," Amanda wrote. "He couldn't risk going through diplomatic channels. This seemed next to impossible. How would a Starfleet officer directly communicate with the chancellor of the Klingon High Council? It's a testimony to my son's logic—and creativity—that he found a way."

The route that Spock took to get to Gorkon was circuitous, but, in the end, quite logical. Spock knew that no one could know of his mission and that included anyone who helped him get in touch with Gorkon. Spock also knew that Curzon Dax had earned the trust of several Klingons. But Spock had never met Curzon Dax—nor would he—and he couldn't expect Dax to help him without explanation. So Spock went to retired Federation President Hiram Roth, who knew both Dax and Spock well. Roth trusted him, and when Spock said he needed Dax to get him in touch with

OFFICE OF THE PRESIDENT

Chancellor Gorkin,

I write you to thank you for your efforts in the past weeks with our representative Captain Spock. As the leader of my government, I have high hopes that the work the two of you have already done will lead to a lasting peace between the Klingon Empire and the Federation.

It is with that in mind I would like to invite you to Earth, on a date that proves convenient to you, so we may begin formal negotiations along the lines that you have already been pursuing. I guarantee safe passage for you and any of your associates you see fit to bring.

I very much look forward to meeting you, so that we may both find a way to end the discord that has bedeviled both our peoples.

Sincerely,

Gorkon, but didn't give a reason, Roth didn't ask why. (The full story behind Spock and Roth's relationship is explored in the short history *Whales Weep Not* by Dr. Gillian Taylor.)

When Roth contacted Dax, Dax didn't ask why either. Dax immediately contacted Kang on a private receiver. Although he was a close friend (Kang had just made Dax godfather to his son), Kang was reticent to help; to put the chancellor of the High Council in direct contact with a Starfleet officer was a risk to his own reputation. But he did it because it was Dax who was asking.

Kang contacted Gorkon, and said he was fulfilling an obligation to a fellow warrior. He provided Gorkon with the personal receiver frequency of a Starfleet officer named Spock. Kang, when telling Dax of it later, said there was a long pause—then Gorkon thanked him. Gorkon was well-informed and intuitive enough to read between the lines: he knew Spock was the son of the Vulcan ambassador to the Federation Council, and that this was a subtle diplomatic outreach.

"My father knew that the imminent threat," wrote Azetbur, Gorkon's daughter, in the tome of heroes in the Klingon Hall of Warriors, "was not from without, but from within. He knew we had to take what we used for war and turn it to life!"

According to Klingon honor, however, any attempt to scale back the military would be a sign of weakness; Gorkon would be immediately challenged and probably killed. "But my father saw through the veil of lies of those around him who spoke only of the need to attack, to kill, to die, and he remembered the words of Kahless: destroying an Empire to win a war is no victory. And ending a battle to save an Empire is no defeat."

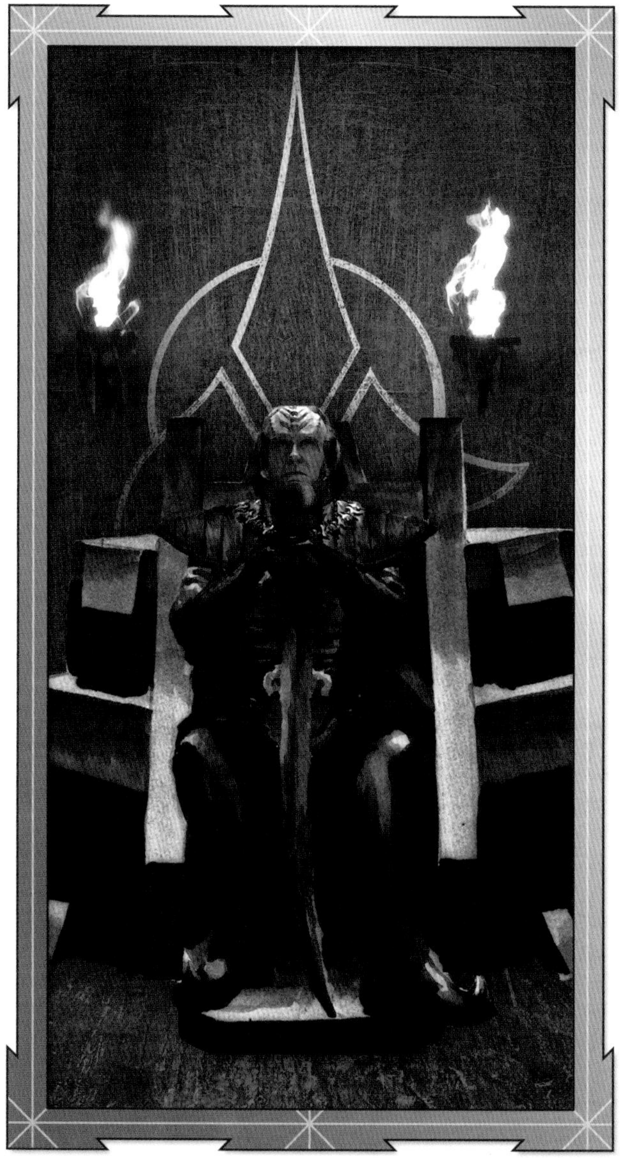

Gorkon contacted Spock via subspace radio. When they spoke, Spock laid out the problems that Gorkon already knew he faced. Gorkon did not deny any of it; he remained silent. Spock recounted in his report to Sarek that he took

ABOVE: Chancellor Gorkon.

Gorkon's silence to mean assent, but also knew he would have to offer him something. He carefully continued and said: "There are many in the Federation to whom scaling back of our own military obligations would be agreeable."

Gorkon was silent, then asked, "Are you one of those people?"

Spock replied, "I am." Gorkon said he appreciated Spock's thoughts, and ended the conversation.

Spock was unsure whether he had made any progress until Gorkon contacted him again the next day. Spock remembered him simply saying, "My people are not surrendering. If it is ever said that we are, then we will fight you to the last warrior." Spock replied that he understood.

With that, the two began the negotiations that Spock would ultimately bring to the Federation Council. He would tell them that Gorkon was ready to come to Earth to begin formal peace negotiations to simultaneously dissolve the Neutral Zone and dismantle the space stations and starbases on both sides, returning to the '67 borders before the Organian Peace Treaty.

The Federation Council ordered Starfleet to arrange a rendezvous with a Klingon ship to bring Gorkon back to Earth. But Starfleet knew that this was only the beginning. Once the negotiations were public, Starfleet was certain that there would be rogue Klingon elements who would do everything they could to undermine the peace process. But it would turn out that it wasn't just Gorkon who would face opposition from within his own government—Starfleet and the Federation would as well.

THE CONSPIRACY

Ambassador Nanclus had been busy. His spy network on Earth had learned about the peace initiative, and he knew what his government's reaction would be before he heard it: peace between the Klingons and the Federation was unacceptable. It would create a shift in the balance of power in the quadrant that would leave the Romulans at a severe disadvantage. He devised a conspiracy, the full story of which was presented by one of his co-conspirators, Admiral Cartwright, during his trial for treason.

"Nanclus was given the order to undermine the treaty however he could," Admiral Cartwright said, "and frankly, his honesty about his motivation to prevent a united Federation and Klingon Empire earned my trust."

Having spent several years on Earth, Nanclus had gotten to know many officers in Starfleet. And he had a well-placed spy on Cartwright's staff: Lieutenant Laura Mogel

---

FOLLOWING SPREAD: The conspirators who sought to destroy the peace negotiations between the Klingons and the Federation were careful to cover their tracks. There is only one surviving document connected with the conspiracy: a gift request of Romulan Ambassador Nanclus to his government. Nanclus had the tacit, but not official, approval of his government, which wanted to be kept informed of his progress. We now know that this request for permission to buy a birthday present for Federation President Ra-ghoratreii was Nanclus's way of telling his superiors who on Earth and on Qo'noS had decided to join Nanclus's conspiracy. (A *teral'n* is an ancient Romulan trident-like weapon.)

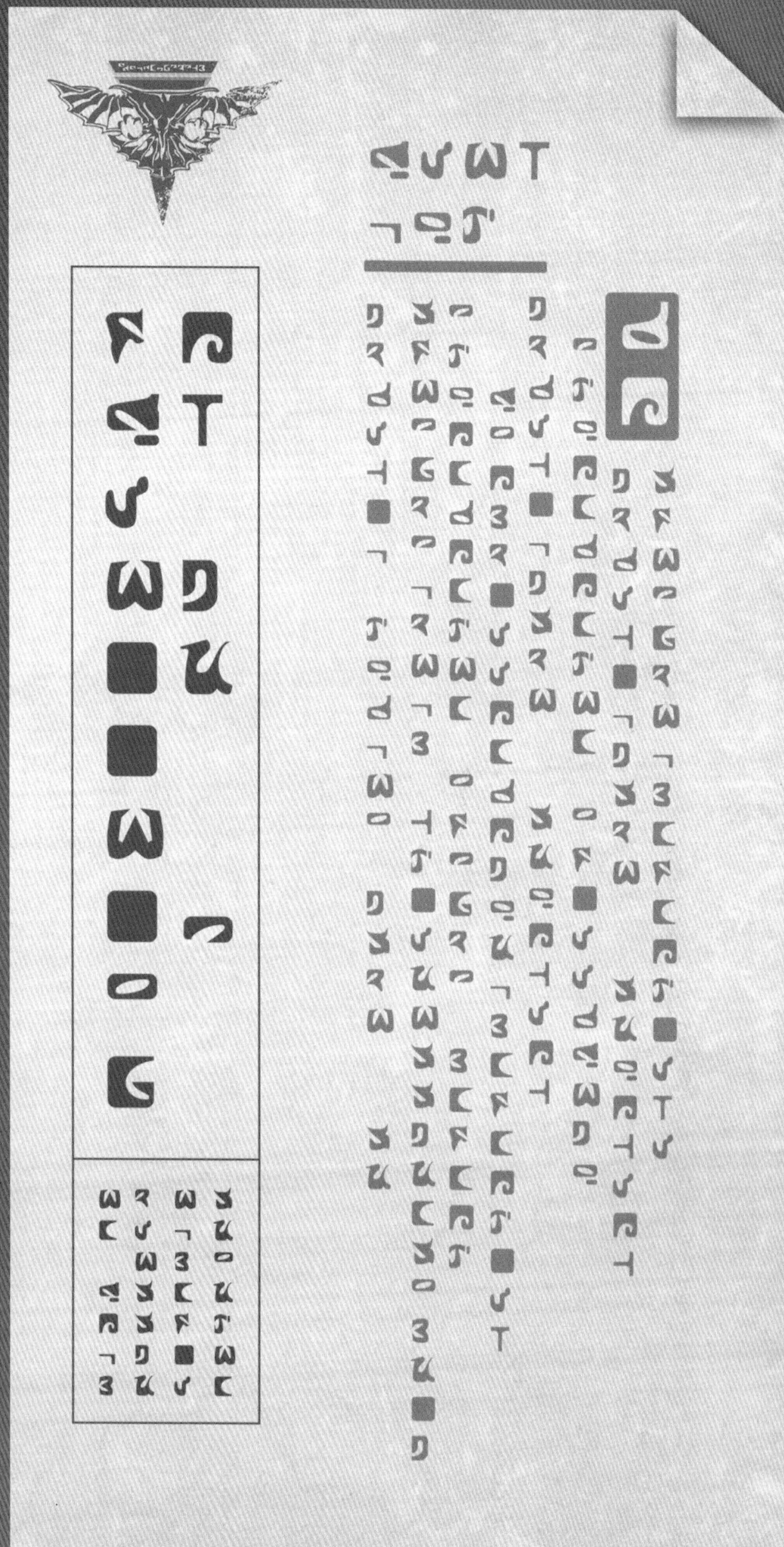

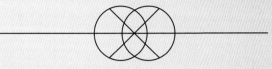

CORRESPONDENCE BETWEEN NANCLUS AND ROMULUS

TRANSLATED FROM THE ROMULAN

5th of T'Lent
A request to the Honorable Director of Romulan Diplomatic Affairs
From his Honor Nanclus, Ambassador to the Federation Council

I am requesting special dispensation to acknowledge the birth of Federation President Ra-ghoratreii with a gift of a *teral'n*. The celebration of the President's birthday is a custom observed on Earth, and I have been informed that many Federation Ambassadors present gifts from their government to the President.

At a state dinner recently, I had a conversation with Admiral Cartwright of Starfleet, who relayed to me that the President is an aficionado of alien weaponry, which led me to the thought that an ancient Romulan weapon would be appropriate. When I was stationed on Qo'noS, you may remember, I made a similar presentation to General Chang, in honor of his long interest in concerns of Romulan/Klingon affairs.

If you approve, I would ask that a *teral'n* be removed from the Romulan State Museum and shipped on the next diplomatic courier.

Nanclus
Ambassador to the Federation Council

had started her life as a Romulan but had been surgically altered to pass as a Human. Nanclus used her first to gain information about Cartwright's point of view, and then to communicate directly to him.

"When Nanclus first got in touch with me, I had no idea how the messages were getting to me; they would just appear on my personal viewscreen," Cartwright said. "And as the plot moved forward, I decided I didn't want to know who Nanclus's go-between was.

"After serving several years as Starfleet commander-in-chief, I had stepped down," Cartwright said in his testimony. "The science and exploratory missions did not interest me." He was put in charge of the security of the Federation, specifically the border with the Klingon Empire.

"I saw what the Klingons were planning, the buildup in ships . . . our way of life was in danger. Our leaders had forgotten what it was like without a Neutral Zone, but I hadn't. I couldn't let it come down." So when Nanclus said he had a suggestion on how to keep the Neutral Zone, Cartwright listened.

Nanclus, before coming to Earth, had served in the Romulan spy service, running agents in the Klingon Empire. He used old contacts to bring General Chang into his conspiracy. "He knew Chang hated Gorkon but Chang needed Starfleet's help to kill him. He knew that if a Klingon did it, it could start a civil war," said Cartwright.

To carry out the assassination, Nanclus needed to know which ship would accompany Gorkon to Earth, and he needed personnel to carry out the assassination. "I gave him everything he needed; I had given orders to kill people before," Cartwright said. "I believed the alternative was worse."

THE ASSASSINATION

When William Smillie, the Starfleet commander-in-chief, informed his officers about the peace initiative, Cartwright pretended he was hearing about it for the first time. By that time, however, the conspiracy was well under way. He voiced his opposition to the peace initiative as he knew his feelings about the Klingons were too well known for him to feign support. Until that meeting, however, he did not know that the *U.S.S. Enterprise* was going to escort Gorkon to Earth; he considered it a bit of luck that Captain Kirk also voiced his opposition to the mission.

"I had gathered a small cadre of officers and crew whom I knew I could trust, and I arranged for their transfer to the *Enterprise*," said Cartwright.

One day into the mission, Cartwright's team carried out Gorkon's assassination. False evidence planted by the collaborators led the Klingons to believe Captain Kirk and his chief medical officer, McCoy, were responsible.

"My hatred of Klingons went back a long way," Kirk said. "I had a lot of enemies in the Empire. I could see why they thought it was me."

Upon Gorkon's death, his daughter Azetbur was appointed in his place. She said she wanted to continue her father's work, but she also wanted revenge for his death. At this point, the entire peace process might have fallen apart—but for the work of Curzon Dax.

If Kirk was executed, Dax felt the door would be permanently closed to a lasting peace. So he had his friend Koloth arrange a meeting with the new chancellor. Azetbur had heard of Curzon Dax, whose name was becoming legendary among the Klingons. Dax, in a report to the Federation

Council, said that when he initially met with Azetbur, the execution of Kirk was a foregone conclusion. "But I asked her the question," Dax said, "would her father want Kirk executed?" When he left her, Dax did not know what the outcome would be, but Kirk's and McCoy's death sentences were commuted to life imprisonment on the penal asteroid of Rura Penthe. Azetbur also expressed her commitment to continue the peace conference.

"This was not the outcome we were looking for," Cartwright testified. The assassination had not ended the peace process. "And with Kirk in prison, another attempt on the Klingon chancellor would show he hadn't acted alone, which was the narrative we'd constructed. We had to come up with a new plan."

The location for a new peace conference was to be on Khitomer, a neutral planet near the Romulan Neutral Zone. "We decided to assassinate the Federation president," Cartwright said, "and make it look like a Klingon was taking revenge for the death of Gorkon."

Spock, who had taken command of the *Enterprise* upon the arrest of Captain Kirk, knew that his longtime friends had nothing to do with the assassination of Gorkon and believed that there was some kind of conspiracy. In direct violation of orders, he crossed the Klingon frontier and

ABOVE: Captain Kirk and the *U.S.S. Enterprise*'s Chief Medical Officer Leonard McCoy on trial for the assassination of Chancellor Gorkon.

rescued Kirk and McCoy from Rura Penthe. "Azetbur had said that any such act would be considered an act of war," Kirk said. "Spock gambled that we'd be able to uncover the conspiracy before she noticed. I was lucky that I worked with a Vulcan who gambled."

Enterprise arrived at Khitomer, and Kirk, Spock, and their crew (with the assistance of the crew of the *U.S.S. Excelsior*, under the command of Hikaru Sulu) were able to prevent the assassination of Ra-ghoratreii. General Chang was killed, Cartwright and Nanclus arrested. And with these acts, Azetbur and her fellow Klingons saw firsthand the evidence of not only the conspiracy, but the true honor of the members of Starfleet and the Federation.

THE KHITOMER ACCORDS

Though the Klingon Empire would not be folded into the Federation, the Khitomer Accords would afford them a unique status. First and foremost, the United Federation of Planets granted and guaranteed the humanitarian aid necessary to overcome the disaster caused by the destruction of Praxis. The Accords also ordered the immediate opening of the border between the Empire and the Federation and the dismantling of the bases between them.

Beyond the immediate crisis, the Accords gave the Klingons the benefits of completely open trade agreements between the Federation members, and established formal channels to resolve differences between the Klingons and any member. The Klingons were also given a non-voting seat on the Federation Council, which would allow them access and consultation on internal matters of the United Federation of Planets. The Accords allowed for the Klingons to maintain their own defense force, but also gave them the protection of Starfleet if they faced a common enemy. Also, both Starfleet and the Klingon fleet agreed to joint military education (although, as of this writing, no Klingon has ever taken the Federation up on its open offer to apply for admission to Starfleet Academy).

Like the formation of the Federation itself, the Khitomer Accords began a new age. The Klingons and the Federation took their first real steps to a genuine, lasting peace. (Though the crisis in the Klingon Empire put much of the Accords into effect immediately, the final document is—to this day—still being negotiated.)

The Romulans, whose ambassador was expelled from Earth following the conspiracy, returned to their isolationist policies, and withdrew behind the Neutral Zone.

OPPOSITE: The Federation President Ra-ghoratreii and Azetbur, the chancellor of the Klingon Empire, began building the longest lasting peace the two age-old enemies had ever known. The details of the diplomatic document were complex and took years to hammer out. It was clear from the beginning that paranoia still existed within the two governments; one of the articles concerned a guarantee that the parties would never join in a war against each other, and that all past grievances were to be officially forgotten. Article V is also of interest, as it made clear to both Federation citizens and Klingons, who still bore the scars of years of hostility, that they'd be turned over to their enemy if they ever acted on such feelings. Only a small portion of the signatures are reproduced here; they went on at some length, as every member world of the Federation sent a delegate who signed it.

THE ACCORDS OF PEACE AND MUTUAL COOPERATION
between
THE KLINGON EMPIRE AND THE UNITED FEDERATION OF PLANETS

The Council of the United Federation of Planets and the High Council of the Klingon Empire, desirous of strengthening the cause of peace between them, have reached the following agreement:

ARTICLE I—Both Parties obligate themselves to desist from any act of violence, any aggressive action, and any attack on each other, either individually or jointly with other powers.

ARTICLE II—The Governments of the two Parties shall institute full diplomatic relations with each other. A parcel of land shall be delivered on each of the worlds, which will serve as the center of government for each Party so that the other Party may establish an Embassy.

ARTICLE III—Should one of the Parties become the object of belligerent action by a third power, the other Party shall in no manner lend its support to this third power, and will lend whatever aid and assistance to the other party it deems appropriate by the rules of its internal government.

ARTICLE IV—Both Parties agree to provide humanitarian aid to each other.

ARTICLE V—Both Parties agree that any former grievances they had with the other are now forgotten. If any individual under the rule of one Party commits an act of revenge or retribution on the other Party, that individual will be extradited to stand trial under the laws of the aggrieved Party.

ARTICLE VI—Both Parties agree to the specifics of the following sections delineating conflict resolution, territorial definitions, trade laws, and all other provisions in this document.

Done, in the English, Vulcan, Klingon, Andorian, Tellarite languages,

Signed,

Ra-ghoratreii
President
United Federation of Planets

Azetbur
Chancellor
Klingon High Council

Eulogy for James T. Kirk

James Tiberius Kirk, the man we come here to mourn, taught me many things. One of the most important was the Human concept of humor, something he valued highly, and he would not want me to ignore the irony of this unique situation I have found myself in, of delivering a eulogy for the man who delivered my eulogy. I am, to use a Human term, "returning the favor."

Although raised in Iowa, Kirk was the child of two Starfleet officers. It seemed natural that he would pursue a career in Starfleet. In another reality, would he have had the same goals? It is impossible to know for certain, but there was something about Starfleet and James T. Kirk that seemed inexorably intertwined.

The youngest man ever to command a starship, he was never egotistical about this accomplishment, and he was always aware of the responsibilities. He once described himself as a soldier, not a diplomat, but he was both. He was a man of peace who knew how to fight; he was thoughtful but decisive, willing to admit his mistakes, and determined to learn from them.

His life was primarily about the life he encountered, learning about it, saving it, appreciating its value. He considered this his greatest responsibility. He protected the citizens of the Federation, the crew who served with him, and each new species he discovered. His actions saved the lives of countless people. Most recently, he saved the lives of millions by preventing an intergalactic war with the Klingons. And then, perhaps appropriately, he died saving lives.

He was our greatest hero, and it will be an adjustment to learn to continue without his help. But the Federation will go on, due in no small part to his efforts. I am honored to have served with him, but, more importantly to me, I am happy to have had him as my first friend.

2311:150 YEARS OF THE FEDERATION

For the two months leading up to October 11, 2311, the Sol system opened itself up to the Galaxy and welcomed aliens from across the Milky Way for the sesquicentennial anniversary of the founding of the United Federation of Planets. Sporting events, dramatic reenactments, technological demonstrations, scientific and cultural exchanges, award presentations, and an endless number of celebrations were capped off with the admission of the eighty first member, Betazed. It felt—at least for a moment—that the Galaxy was one.

248 years before, the Alpha Quadrant looked vastly different. Earth, a primitive planet, was on the verge of a permanent dark age, Vulcan had slipped into imperialism, and the major races of Andoria, Tellar, Klingon, and Romulus were free to take advantage of the weaker worlds they encountered. Because of a chance meeting between a Human and a Vulcan, the people of these worlds—and many others—were put on a road to civilization, democracy, and a continual hope for the future.

And on the spot where that first meeting took place, one of the participants returned. At 308 years old, Solkar is long-lived even for a Vulcan. He had not returned to Earth since he left his position as ambassador in the early twenty-second century.

In a short speech to a huge crowd of people who had gathered in Montana—and millions more watching via subspace—Solkar spoke of his Human counterpart:

"It is not generally known," Solkar said, "but due to my species' natural telepathic gifts, when Cochrane and I first shook hands, our minds briefly touched. It created a link between us . . . a link that should have ended when he died. But it did not. I am still aware of it, aware of his mind lurking somewhere, off on a distant world. There are two logical explanations. The first is our link left in my mind a touch of the Human desire to accept the superstition of an afterlife. The second is, Zefram Cochrane is not dead. I find either explanation acceptable. The first serves as a reminder of the diversity of spirit that has allowed this Federation to flourish. The second would mean that my friend Zefram is here with me now, and knows what our meeting has wrought."

OPPOSITE: The eulogy for James T. Kirk was given by his closest friend, Spock. Captain Kirk died aboard the *U.S.S. Enterprise*-B after saving it from destruction inside a temporal nexus. It is an informally accepted fact that if there was one person who shaped the century he lived in, it was Kirk.

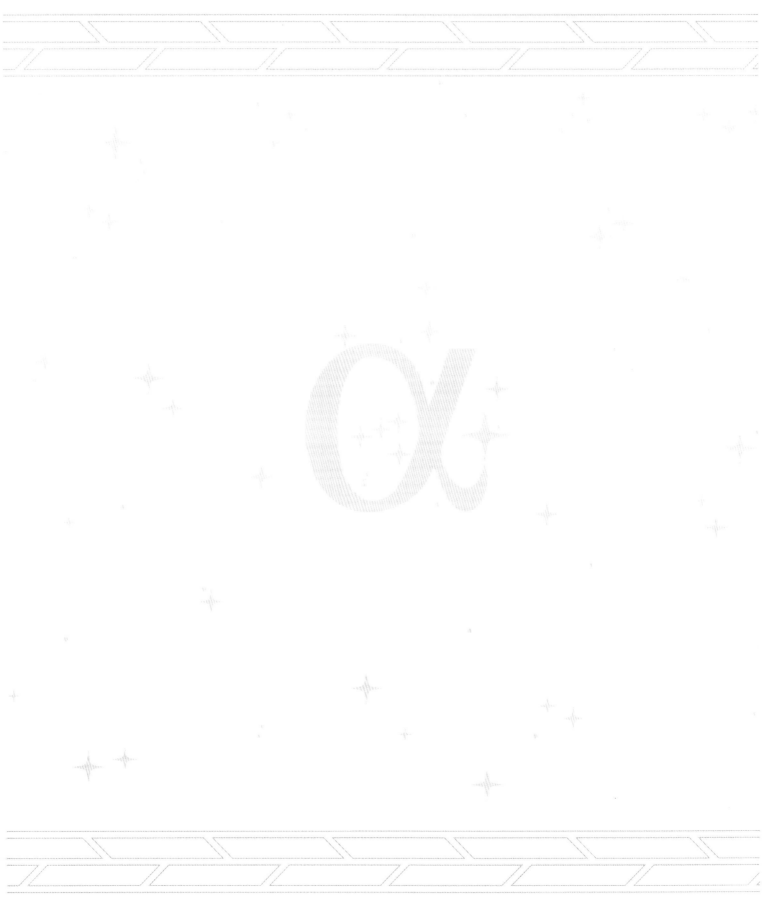

SELECTED BIBLIOGRAPHY

Aleek Om, Loom. *Changing Spots: Klingons in the 23rd Century.* Aurelian University Press, 33092 (Aurelian Calendar).

April, Robert, ed. *History of the Development and Construction of the Constitution-Class Ships.* Starfleet Academy Library, Memory Alpha.

Archer, Henry. "Design and Development Necessities of a Warp Five Engine." PhD Dissertation, State University of New York at Albany, 2118.

Archer, Jonathan. "Who We Were and Who We Are." Speech to Starfleet Academy Graduating Class, San Francisco, CA, 18 June 2199.

Dax, Curzon. *Report on the Korvat Talks.* Federation Diplomatic Archive, Memory Alpha.

DeLongpre, Allen Gregory. "The Brave New World of Andrew Paul Mitchell." *Orlando Post Dispatch,* 23 June 2069, Section A:1.

Dowling-Goodman, Joshua and Steven, eds. *Official History of Starfleet Academy.* San Francisco: Starfleet Academy Press, 2290.

Erickson, Danica. *A Beaming Parent: How My Father's Invention Changed Space Travel.* New Chicago: University of Chicago Press, 2170.

Gileus I. Unpublished Journal. Romulan Document Archive, Memory Alpha.

Gill, John. *Small Steps and Giant Leaps: A History of Humankind in the Galaxy.* San Francisco: Starfleet Academy Press, 2143.

——. *World War III: A History.* San Francisco: Starfleet Academy Press, 2120.

Grayson, Amanda. *Love and Logic.* London: Fontana Books, 2297.

Griffin, Brian. *First Captain: A Biography of Jonathan Archer.* Quahog: Pewterschmidt Press, 2255.

J'Acov. *The Great Diaspora: The History of the Xindi.* The Xindi Memorial Project, Memory Alpha.

James, Dasheill, and Francesca Lucia, eds. *The Great Experiment: The Oral History of the Construction and Voyage of the S.S. Conestoga.* Davida Rossi Foundation Archives, December 2079.

Matalas, Terence, ed. *History of the Warp 5 Project*. Starfleet Command Archives, Memory Alpha.

Mindar. Right of Statement. Romulan Document Archive, Memory Alpha.

Paskey, Edward. *A Piece of the Action: The Unique Case of Sigma Iotia II.* London: Gene Harmon Press, 2179.

Proceedings of the United Earth Council Meeting, May 18, 2156. American Continent Institute Archive, Memory Alpha.

Papers of Matthew Root. The Thomas Senreich European Hegemony Library, Titan Maximum Colony.

Samuel, Jacob. "Dr. Archer, Meet Dr. Cochrane," *Albany Times-Union,* 18 August 2122, pgs. 1, 3.

Samuels, Nathan. Unpublished Memoirs. Nathan Samuels Foundation Library, Sunnydale, California.

Sanchez, Manuel. *Official Biography of James T. Kirk.* San Francisco: Starfleet Academy Press, 2307.

Scully, Brian. "Farmer Shoots Alien," *Springfield Shopper,* 2 April 2063, pg. 3.

Shran, Thy'lek. *Memoirs.* Andorian High Command Press, 6180 (Andorian Calendar).

Papers of Soval. Ambassador to Earth. Diplomatic Archives, ShiKahr, Vulcan.

Sulkin, Alexa. *Light Speed: The Life of Zefram Cochrane.* Boston: Wellesley Press, 2160.

Surak. *Recollections.* Vulcan Science Academy, 8891 (Vulcan Calendar).

Syran. *The Teachings of Surak.* Vulcan Science Academy Library, 8769 (Vulcan Calendar).

Taylor, Gillian. *Whales Weep Not: My 300-Year Voyage Home with George and Gracie.* San Francisco: Bennett Press, 2299.

T'Pol. *Personal Logs*. Starfleet Crew Logs, Memory Alpha.

Report of Vulcan High Command to the Vulcan High Council Regarding the Disposition of the Self-Described Planet Earth. Vulcan Science Academy Library, 8660 (Vulcan Calendar).

Report on the Incident Involving the Klingon Klaang Return to Qo'noS. Ambassador to Earth, Vulcan High Command Archives, Memory Alpha.

Van Citters, Liam, and Nicholas Counter, eds. *Living Witness History of Tarsus IV.* Federation History Archives, Memory Alpha.

Vanderbilt, Thomas. *The Founding: First Days of Federation.* New Rochelle: The Julia Emma Press, 2197.

Vebber, Eric. *Hodgkin's Law: How Termites Explained the Galaxy.* New New York: Planet Express Publications, 2170.

———, ed. *Report on the Origins of the Klingon Hostility Toward Earth.* 2174, Federation Science Council Archive, Memory Alpha.

ABOUT THE AUTHOR

David A. Goodman was born in New Rochelle, New York. After graduating from the University of Chicago, he moved to Los Angeles in 1988 to write on the television sitcom *The Golden Girls*. Since then Goodman has written for over fifteen television series, including *Wings*, *Dream On*, *Star Trek: Enterprise*, and *Futurama* (for which he wrote the Nebula Award–nominated *Star Trek* homage "Where No Fan Has Gone Before"). But he is probably best known for his work on *Family Guy*, for which he served as head writer and executive producer for six years and over one hundred episodes. He lives in Pacific Palisades, California, with his family. This is his first book.

ABOUT THE ILLUSTRATORS

Joe Corroney has provided Lucasfilm with official *Star Wars* artwork for books, games, trading cards, comic books, posters and magazines since 1997. He's illustrated other comic books including *Star Trek, GI Joe, Fallen Angel, 24: Nightfall, Doctor Who, Angel,* and *Spike vs. Dracula* for IDW Publishing. Corroney is currently illustrating for IDW's new *True Blood* series and BOOM! Studios' *Farscape* comic books, developing his creator owned comic book series, *Death Avenger* and continuing to create new *Star Wars* artwork for Lucasfilm.

Mark McHaley is an artist and commercial illustrator. His corporate clients include Disney, Kraft, Golden Books, and various others. Currently, he creates illustrations for properties held by Marvel, DC, Lucasfilm, 5finity, and more.

Cat Staggs has illustrated more than 130 cards for the *Star Wars: Revenge of the Sith* card set and works for Lucasfilm. She has produced exclusive prints for *Star Wars* Celebrations III, IV, and Europe, and has also illustrated short fiction for starwars.com. In addition, Cat works in the comic books and film genres, and she has completed card sets for *The Lord of the Rings, Marvel Avengers, X-Men,* and *DC Legacy*, among others.

Jeff Carlisle is a lifelong *Star Trek* fan and freelance illustrator/concept designer for properties including *Star Wars, Dungeons & Dragons, Pathfinder, Indiana Jones, Lord of the Rings, Doctor Who,* and *The Guild*. His work has appeared across many platforms, including books, magazines, trading cards, posters, art prints, and even paper airplanes.

ACKNOWLEDGMENTS

First and foremost, thank you, Dave Rossi, for your unexpected phone call to write this book, and John Van Citters at CBS Consumer Products for listening to Dave and hiring me. And thank you both for invaluable help on the manuscript. Also thanks to: Mike Sussman, Chris Black, Brannon Braga, and Paula Block for your notes and support; my three editors: Amelia Riedler, whose initial contributions were vital in shaping this project; Kristin Mehus-Roe, who had the unenviable task of making me deliver on deadline and who did an incredible amount of work whipping the manuscript into shape; and Dana Youlin, who had to step in at the end to wrap this up. Also, Gabe Stromberg for his incredible designs, Todd Rider for that pedestal (and George Takei for showing up to record Admiral Sulu), and Tom Miller for all the production work.

When I started writing this book, I was partially inspired by an old book I had in high school, *The Star Trek Spaceflight Chronology*, my copy of which I passed on to my younger brother Rafael in 1984. My hope is he doesn't lose this copy. Also, thank you to my sisters Naomi Press and Ann Goodman, and my mother, Brunhilde Goodman, for only rolling their eyes but never making me actually turn off *Star Trek* until it was over. Finally, my children Jacob and Talia, and my wife, Wendy, who are really the only reasons I do anything.

IMAGE CREDITS

Page 16: American eagle stamp © hypedesign/Shutterstock

Page 18: Old paper sheet © Tischenko Irina/Shutterstock; red wax seal © Iznogood/Shutterstock

Page 24: Scale of justice © Thank You/Shutterstock

Page 54: Old paper © Anan Kaewkhammul/Shutterstock

Page 69: Old cotton texture © Ra Studio/Shutterstock

Page 89: Eagle with sword, laurel, and ribbon © BVA/Shutterstock

Special features: Perforated computer paper © Feng Yu/Shutterstock; ancient manuscript © Roman Sigaev/Shutterstock; computer paper © c./Shutterstock; aged scroll paper © photostudio 7/Shutterstock; scroll of old paper with curled edges © Chyrko Olena/Shutterstock; old paper isolated on white © Valentin Agapov/Shutterstock; old paper isolated on white © Sailorr/Shutterstock; postmark and stamp © Hudyma Natallia/Shutterstock

STAR TREK®

Federation: The First 150 Years

ISBN: 9781781169155

Published by
Titan Books
A division of Titan Publishing Group Ltd.
144 Southwark St.
London
SE1 0UP

First edition: October 2013

2 4 6 8 10 9 7 5 3 1

Federation: The First 150 Years was published by arrangement with becker&mayer!

Editors: Kristin Mehus-Roe and Dana Youlin
Designers: Gabriel Stromberg and Rosanna Brockley
Production coordinator: Tom Miller
Managing editor: Amelia Riedler
Consulting and research: Chris Munson
Consulting and design assistance: Aileen Morrow
Design assistance: Greg Cook

A CIP catalogue record for this title is available from the British Library.

Printed and bound in China.